The Gospel as Conversation

The Gospel as Conversation

Texts, Sermons, and Questions for Reflection

A Study Guide

JAMES BOYD WHITE

WIPF & STOCK · Eugene, Oregon

THE GOSPEL AS CONVERSATION
Texts, Sermons, and Questions for Reflection
A Study Guide

Copyright © 2013 James Boyd White. All rights reserved. Except for brief quotations in critical publications or reviews, no part of this book may be reproduced in any manner without prior written permission from the publisher. Write: Permissions. Wipf and Stock Publishers, 199 W. 8th Ave., Suite 3, Eugene, OR 97401.

Unless otherwise indicated, all scriptural quotations are from the New Revised Standard Version Bible, copyright © 1989 National Council of the Churches of Christ in the United States of America. Used by permission. All rights reserved.

Wipf & Stock
An Imprint of Wipf and Stock Publishers
199 W. 8th Ave., Suite 3
Eugene, OR 97401

www.wipfandstock.com

ISBN 13: 978-1-62564-016-1

Manufactured in the U.S.A.

*In thanks for the poetry of George Herbert,
which transformed my life*

Contents

Foreword | ix
Preface | xiii
Acknowledgments | xv
Introduction | xvii

1. A Prophet Not without Honor | 1
2. "Many of His Disciples Turned Back" | 8
3. Trust and Fear | 15
4. The Widow's Mite | 22
5. The Temptation of Jesus | 28
6. Amos and the Good Samaritan | 36
7. The Woman in the Synagogue | 44
8. Lazarus and Dives | 50
9. The Pharisee and the Tax Collector | 57
10. The Annunciation to Joseph | 64
11. Abraham and Nicodemus | 71
12. "I Am in My Father, and You in Me, and I in You" | 80
13. "I Am with You Always, to the End of the Age" | 87
14. Jesus' Imagistic Thinking | 96
15. Living Together in Unity | 103
16. Suffering | 111
17. "Keep Awake" | 119
18. "The Kingdom of God Has Come Near" | 126
19. The Transfiguration of Jesus | 133
20. Palm Sunday | 139
21. "Love One Another as I Have Loved You" | 147
22. Jesus' Healing | 154

23	"Who Then Is This?"	161
24	"Whoever Believes Has Eternal Life"	167
25	"You Are the Messiah"	173
26	The Rich Young Man	180
27	Christ the King	187
28	Repent or Perish	193
29	The Resurrection of Jesus	200
30	Jesus in the Locked Room	208

Foreword

Papa, don't preach.
—Madonna

Just what is a sermon? What is this "preaching" we don't want to hear from a "Papa," especially when we, like Madonna's protagonist, are "in trouble deep"? Preaching is not defined by its content. Preachers well known enough to surely exemplify the field—John Donne, Jonathan Edwards, Phillips Brooks, William Spurgeon, Billy Graham, Martin Luther King Jr., William Sloane Coffin, Jerry Falwell, Norman Vincent Peale, William Willimon—have said strikingly different things. So it isn't the content that Madonna's protagonist cringes away from like a blow but a style, a genre, a dogmatic proclamation that feels like a literary assault.

The form and style of sermons matter because they express more of the preacher's image of God than does the content of the message. I suspect the form and style of sermons also shapes the congregation's view of God more than does the content of the message. If preaching is something we do not want to hear when we are "in trouble deep," then that preaching is not portraying a God who is "a very present help in time of trouble."

If preaching means sanctimonious moralizing or dogmatic exhortation to do this or not do that, then James Boyd White is no preacher. That isn't what he does. His sermons do not assault the conscience but invite the imagination. So I ask: what kind of God is White portraying in these sermons? Don't look at the content. Look at the questioning, conversational, invitational form of his sermons. Then suppose: God does not throw a lightning bolt at me to get my attention, then thunder commandments, but instead comes as a still, small voice of curiosity. What kind of God would approach me in this way? What kind of God would instead thunder the commandments? What kind of God would berate me with sanctimonious moralizing? If God is the most beautiful, the most true, the highest value, the greatest good, then what kind of God do I believe in? White's presentation of the gospel message, by its very difference in style, invites us to reconsider who God is—and that is the ultimate foundational question.

In *The Gospel as Conversation*, the noted legal scholar James Boyd White starts his reading of a gospel passage with the bare-bones skeleton of the story it tells and, like a good lawyer, starts asking questions. He wonders about the all-important details. If the details are so important, why were they left out? Perhaps to invite us to fill them in. Maybe we get to write the important parts. White focuses on what the text doesn't say. He engages his religious imagination to fill in the blanks and make the meaning. But he never claims his imaginative engagement with the text is the only right way to read it. He uses his imagination to model how we might do the same thing, how we might fill in the blanks and find meaning for ourselves.

Each sermon—which is an imaginative infilling of details leading to creative interpretation—is preceded by questions for the reader to ask of the text. White invites us to engage the story for ourselves before hearing his reading of it. Then, after showing us how he has worked with the lesson, there are more questions for us to ponder.

This book is an extended exercise in conversational wonder. The text speaks a little. We ask questions. We answer with our imaginations. White shares his imaginative expansion of the story and his interpretation. Then we ask questions about how best to interpret the story and we engage our reason to interpret the gospel lesson for ourselves. Of course, we can spiral on into interpreting White's interpretation. It is ongoing.

The Gospel as Conversation is a heartening book. The content of the sermons is excellent, but the content is not the point. The point is the conversational style of the sermons. The style is crucial for two reasons. The first reason is theological. The God I believe in is conversational, invitational—not coercive, not domineering, not bombastic. My belief in this relational God is not a personal idiosyncrasy. Christians have known this God for centuries. Ancient and medieval ways of prayer assumed just such a God. St. Ignatius of Loyola designed the Spiritual Exercises around just such imaginative dialogue. The religious imagination was considered to be a part of the faculty of reason by means of which it is possible to know something of God. The problem is that most Christians had no access to these prayer disciplines. The God they knew was the one they met in sermons, which sadly did not often reflect the same God they knew in prayer. The structure of the sermon overrode the prayer experience. So the relational God was lost in a din of homilies. Perhaps that is where the split between spirituality and religion began.

The second reason *The Gospel as Conversation* is heartening is both ethical and spiritual. This way of reading the lessons can make us better people precisely because it invites us to imagine the experience of other human beings confronted with the challenges of life, God, right and wrong, hard and easy. The interpretive process begins and ends with engaging our capacity to see the world through someone else's eyes.

In her recent book *The New Religious Intolerance*, philosopher Martha Nussbaum argues that the fear that afflicts so many of us today is a primitive, narcissistic emotion that constricts our thoughts and feelings to an anxious struggle to keep ourselves safe. Fear shrinks our world, diminishes our lives. Nussbaum says fear is natural but it gets culturally focused and amplified in irrational ways that prevent us from exercising our moral imaginations. But that is not natural or necessary. "More generally," she says, "the imagination makes others real for us. A common human failing is to see the whole world from the point of view of one's own goals, and to see the conduct of others as all about oneself. . . . By imagining other people's way of life, we don't necessarily learn to agree with their goals; but we do see the reality of those goals for them. We learn that other worlds of thought and feeling exist." In order to discover those worlds, she suggests that we deliberately cultivate "participatory imagination"—the ability to imagine our way into someone else's shoes.

The Gospel as Conversation is an exercise in the participatory imagination, placing us in the utterly human context of people who met Jesus, the utterly human context that is the crucible of spiritual transformation. If we exercise the capacity to think what something was like for another, then we develop moral capacity, the capacity for empathy that can expand our world, deepen our lives, and enable us to befriend one another.

The substance of these sermons is relatively less crucial than the conversational process out of which they arise. However, that is not to say that the substance is not intrinsically important and valuable. The message here is rendered the more important by the process that shapes it. A message that is part of a conversation is necessarily different from a message that purports to be the first and final word on any subject. The content of these sermons is decidedly influenced, perhaps determined, by the dialogical context. The result is something truly special. Yes, the voice of these sermons grabs our attention first. But the substance of White's message proves to be consonant with the voice. His sermons are intelligent, compassionate, and gently human. *The Gospel as Conversation* will be a blessing to the Church.

The Rt. Rev. Dan Edwards
Bishop of Nevada

Preface

EACH CHAPTER OF THIS book contains a passage from one of the gospels (and sometimes some of the other readings for the day), a sermon I have given on the passage, and a set of questions for reflection. The idea, as the title suggests, is to invite the reader to engage in his or her version of the conversation that the gospels began two thousand years ago and have kept going ever since. My own version of this conversation is reflected in the sermons themselves, and in the questions I ask. The reader's engagement can be private—just between the reader and the text—or it can take place with others, as in a study group or seminar. In either event, the premise on which the book operates is that the gospels acquire their life and meaning in the conversational process by which we connect with them.

This means that we are responsible for our part in these conversations, for the questions we raise and the responses we offer. We can, of course, trivialize the gospels, say by converting them into sentimental fictions, by trying to turn them to our own advantage, or by treating them as the occasion for the kind of talk we see in a chat room or bull session.

Or we can—well, do what, exactly? What *is* a good kind of conversation to have about the gospels? That is a central question of this book, and what follows is my own best effort to respond to it. I hope you will engage with that question too, answering it in your own way, perhaps in a way that is critical of what I say and do. My hope is that these gospel texts and sermons and questions will be starting points for further thought and discussion, not in any way conclusive. We are all in this together.

These sermons are not scholarly in kind, or meant to defend a theological theory or to assert a position they want the reader to accept. They represent my own engagement with the gospel texts and my own efforts to understand the life to which they call us. They are not an argument for belief, but at best a partial demonstration of what for one person belief has made possible.

Acknowledgments

I WANT TO THANK first of all the Rt. Rev. Wendell Gibbs, who licensed me as a lay preacher in the Diocese of Michigan, and the Rt. Rev. Robert Gepert, who has permitted me to preach at the Church of the Mediator in the Diocese of Western Michigan. I am immensely grateful to both of them for this opportunity, as I am also to the priests who have invited me to preach: the Rev. Alan Gibson, the Rev. Paula Durren, and the Rev. Joseph Summers. Thanks are also due to the congregations of St. Andrew's Church, the Church of the Incarnation, and the Church of the Mediator for their patient and kind acceptance of my efforts.

Many friends have given me generous and unflagging support, and criticism too, especially Walter Brueggemann, Richard Dawson, Howard Lesnick, John McCausland, Bernadette Pelland, Jefferson Powell, Jack Sammons, Lew Towler, Joseph Vining, and above all my wife, Mary. I cannot thank them enough.

I am grateful, too, to the publishers, Wipf and Stock, for doing such a fine job in the production of this book, as they did also with its predecessor, *Connecting to the Gospel*.

Introduction

THIS IS A BOOK about reading the gospels and bringing them into one's own experience of life. It takes the form of passages from the gospels, sermons I have given on those passages, and questions meant to open them up for the reader. My premise throughout is that the gospels cannot be reduced to rules for life, to stories illustrating moral lessons, or to facts demonstrating the truth of theological propositions. Quite the opposite: the gospels are—in my view deliberately—full of problems, uncertainties, tensions, and incompletenesses. These are essential to their meaning. The gospels call on us to engage with them, to read them, to ask questions about them, to live with them alone and together, and in all of this to confront as honestly as we can the difficulties they present. They invite deep and complex responses in us, and it is in those responses that they come to full life.

Thus a passage in one of the gospels may seem to say one thing to us as we first read it; we then discover a question lurking in our minds and bring it back to what we are reading. When we do that we often discover another question, leading to another line of thought. All this suggests the possibility of alternative and contrasting readings, and perhaps connections with other scriptural texts, which themselves ask to be read, and so on in principle indefinitely. At the same time we may well be asking how what we are reading connects to our own lives today and find ourselves mystified or disturbed, looking for resolutions and not finding them.

By this point we are engaged with what we are reading, alone or together, and the life of that engagement is, for the moment, the conversational life of the gospel itself. I think that to say that the gospel lives in conversation is to say that God lives there too. Not in rules and commandments and theological propositions, but in the life that the gospel stimulates in us and calls us to.

This life is different for each person, for each of us has a different soul, a different mind, a different history, and a different location in the world. "How does the gospel speak to me?" is a proper and important question for each of us, and we should expect our answers to be different too. It speaks to each of us in the moment at which we find ourselves. It calls us to bring to our reading and hearing of its words the experience of our actual lives—just as it asks, in turn, to be brought to that experience, to illuminate and perhaps transform it.

It is important that the conversational life to which the gospel calls us is not only that of an individual but that of a community. To read the sacred texts together, over time, has always been the Christian practice, as it has been the Jewish practice too. This reading, and the conversation it generates among us, is in fact one of the ways the church is kept alive. I hope that this book can be read by groups as well as individuals, who will in that way be continuing the conversation that began nearly two thousand years ago. In particular, it is the point of the questions that begin and end each chapter to stimulate conversation within the reader, or among the readers, of this book.

A word about what I mean by *conversation*. I do not mean the kind of casual interchange in which we all engage a good bit of the time, when our brains and souls are turned off, or mutual back scratching, but the opposite of such things, a deep and sometimes fearsome interchange between mind and mind, soul and soul, friend and friend. Questions are an important part of it: questions we ask ourselves; questions we ask each other; and, when we are reading the gospels, questions the gospels put to us. At its best this kind of conversation can lead us out of our familiar terrain into a new space, where new things can be seen and said. We can find ourselves saying things we never knew or heard before. That has certainly been my experience in composing these sermons, and I hope it is your experience too, as you find yourself saying new things in a new way. This is one way the gospels come alive again in our time.

In this book some of the sermons close with a prayer, and some of the questions end by asking you what prayer you would make in response to what you have read. Prayers of both kinds are an important part of our response to the gospels, and an important stage in the conversation they create and guide.

I should also say this: while in one sense the gospels come to us—they reach out to us, they call us into being—in another sense we must go to the gospels, with a readiness to experience the change in ourselves that our engagement with them may bring about. In teaching poetry to undergraduates I found myself saying that a good poem will not simply come to you as you are, offering a feeling or an image you can take away with you, the way, say, an advertisement or political speech does. Rather, it requires you to come to it, to engage with it on its terms, not your own. In this work is its meaning. This is true of the gospels as well, indeed of any text that has as one of its purposes the transformation of its reader.

Deep in the process I am describing is this question: what is the proper relation between the Scripture we are reading and the experience of our own lives, including when we most feel that the Spirit is alive in us and in the world? How can we possibly connect these ancient texts, written in an ancient language, to our lives today? We live in a completely different society, we are formed by a different culture, we engage in different pastimes, we are governed by a different kind of law and polity, we have a radically different experience of the natural world, and we live with a set of technological capacities that could not have been dreamed of in the time of Jesus.

Yet in a deep sense our lives are the same. The gospel is about what is central to human experience. It speaks to our souls.

The sermons are reproduced, with very light editing, in the chronological order in which they were given. They mainly concern the gospel passage for the week, which I reproduce at the beginning of the chapter. Where the sermon discusses one or more of the other readings, I include them as well. Some themes recur, in particular the nature of "belief" and the mysterious nature of the Jesus we read about in Mark's Gospel. Sometimes I include a reference of a highly local kind, for example to a baptism that is about to take place in our church or a stewardship campaign that has just begun. I have left these in as reminders of the particularity of the life to which these sermons are addressed.

I use the general term *gospel* to refer to the general message of Good News that the particular gospel texts in their different ways seek to express. That the gospels are different from each other, creating lines of questioning and tension among them, is in my view one of their great virtues. This fact makes plain that it is our task to engage with the puzzles and difficulties the gospels present, which we cannot expect them to resolve for us. In this they define our responsibility as living and believing and doubting souls.

I encourage you to read the chapters slowly, perhaps only one at a sitting. That will give you time to let the gospel passages live in your mind as invitations to the conversation they exist to invoke.

Let me also add an obvious point, which is that the gospels are the primary texts here. The sermons and questions are offered only as ways of thinking about the gospels and how they might be brought into our lives.

1

A Prophet Not without Honor

In the passage from Mark that follows below we are first told about Jesus' return to his hometown, where he shocked his former townspeople by teaching in the synagogue; then we hear about his commission to his disciples, when he sent them out to preach the Good News of the coming kingdom. What do you suppose these two stories have to do with each other?

As you read this and the other chapters, let me suggest that you take time to be conscious of whatever questions arise in your mind and pay real attention to them. It would be a good idea to have pencil and paper handy, so that you can write them down. Before going further you might ask yourself what you would want to say about the passage, perhaps to a group of like-minded friends.

The idea behind this suggestion is the idea of this whole book, that the gospel gets its full life only as we engage with it, in conversation with ourselves or others.

The Gospel of Mark 6:1–13

He left that place and came to his hometown, and his disciples followed him. On the Sabbath he began to teach in the synagogue, and many who heard him were astounded. They said, "Where did this man get all this? What is this wisdom that has been given to him? What deeds of power are being done by his hands! Is not this the carpenter, the son of Mary and brother of James and Joses and Judas and Simon, and are not his sisters here with us?" And they took offense at him.

Then Jesus said to them, "Prophets are not without honor, except in their hometown, and among their own kin, and in their own house." And he could do no deed of power there, except that he laid his hands on a few sick people and cured them. And he was amazed at their unbelief.

Then he went about among the villages teaching. He called the twelve and began to send them out two by two, and gave them authority over the unclean spirits. He ordered them to take nothing for their journey except a staff; no bread, no bag, no money in their belts; but to wear sandals and not to put on two tunics.

He said to them, "Wherever you enter a house, stay there until you leave the place. If any place will not welcome you and they refuse to hear you, as you leave, shake off the dust that is on your feet as a testimony against them."

So they went out and proclaimed that all should repent. They cast out many demons, and anointed with oil many who were sick and cured them.

The Church of the Mediator, July 4, 2009

May the words of my mouth and the meditations of my heart be always acceptable in thy sight, O Lord, my strength and my redeemer.

Today's gospel contains two seemingly quite different stories: the account of Jesus' return to his hometown, where he is treated with scorn by the people who knew him as a boy; and the moment, a few days later, when he sends out the twelve disciples to preach repentance and cure the sick.

These stories seem to be different, but I think they have a common theme. Let's take them one at a time, starting with the one about Jesus' return to his home.

We learn that when Jesus started teaching in the synagogue it made his former neighbors angry. Why did the people get so angry? It was apparently not because of the substance of what Jesus taught but because he was presuming to teach at all.

Was Jesus in fact doing something improper when he taught in the synagogue? I don't think so. It was certainly not a problem that he was not a rabbi, because his people did not really have rabbis yet—they had "leaders" (like Jairus, whose daughter Jesus healed in another story, which Mark has just told us)—and so far as I know there were no formal requirements for reading and teaching the Scripture in the synagogue.

But there certainly is some problem with Jesus' teaching, for the neighbors react in an extremely hostile way, asking, in effect, "Is this not Mary's son, the carpenter, the brother of these men well known to us, and are these not his sisters?" The men seem to feel that Jesus is not entitled to teach because he is an ordinary person, "just like us." Actually, they make clear that he is worse than they are: when they call him "Mary's son," identifying him only by his mother, they are saying that he has no father at all but is illegitimate. This is the man who is now setting himself up as better than we are, and we, who remember him as a boy, resent it. Who is he to come back and teach us?

Their reaction is extreme, but I think it makes a kind of sense, and does so in an important and disturbing way. It is common in America—maybe you have experienced it?—that someone grows up in a small town, or maybe a city neighborhood, then moves away in early adulthood to lead a life somewhere else, away from his or her family and hometown, and then comes back, years later. What do we expect that return to be like?

There will be curiosity and joy on the part of the family and townspeople; but it is likely that they will also feel some resentment, both at the original departure and at the return. "What was wrong with us? Were we not good enough for you? Why are you coming back now?" The neighbors will also want to pretend that the person is exactly the same person who left, unchanged by time and experience. If he insists that he is different now, they are likely to think he is putting on airs. Old memories, old jokes, old names will be the order of the day.

From the point of view of the person coming home, this can be awful. The neighbors are refusing to recognize who he has become. Surely our traveler will have had all kinds of experiences, have grown and changed, and in the nature of things no longer be the person he once was.

What makes it worse is that the complaint of the community—"Were we not good enough for you?"—has some truth in it. The reason the person went away (and this is true of Jesus) was that there was something he had to do, or become, which he could not do at home. All this is true, but our traveler will still want to affirm the world in which he grew up, which a side of him remembers with deep love.

There is built into such a return kind of deep structural tension. We see it reflected in the title of Thomas Wolfe's famous novel *You Can't Go Home Again.*

The difficulty of "coming home" may help explain not only the hostility of the townspeople, but what to me is the most striking, really astonishing thing, about Mark's story: "And [Jesus] could do no deed of power there, except that he laid his hands on a few sick people and cured them." What can this mean? Why should Jesus, the Son of God, not be able to do whatever deeds of power he wants: miracles and healings and driving out demons and calming storms and feeding thousands of people and raising the dead?

I think Mark is saying that Jesus experiences the tension I have described—the impossibility of coming home—so powerfully that he is partly disabled by it. When he is with these people from his childhood, who refuse to recognize who he is, he cannot fully be the person he has become. Even the Son of God needs his people to recognize him, to have faith in him, if he is to be fully who he is.

As a human matter—and Jesus is human as well as divine—this makes perfect sense. It is true of each of us, all of our lives: our capacity to be who we are is profoundly dependent upon those around us.

Think of the child who is raised by parents who think that there is no such thing as love, or that only winning counts—getting grades or touchdowns or prizes—or who always regard the child as inherently bad, as sneaky and manipulative. Think of the African American child being looked at with overt mistrust by the storekeeper, who thinks that "they" are all thieves. Think of what it is like to work at a job where one's boss and fellow employees think you cannot really do it.

Or think of the opposite of these things: the child whose parents nurture him or her in love, believing that love is the most important thing in the world, much more important than status or money; or parents who do not focus on their child's winning and losing, but on the meaning of who the child is, and what he or she does; or shopkeepers who know how to distinguish on some other ground than race between the trustworthy and untrustworthy child; or the boss and fellow employees who understand and welcome your contribution to your joint work.

In the first kind of situation we are likely to be disabled, damaged, unable to be our full selves, maybe permanently so; in the other case, we flower and grow, becoming perhaps someone we would never have dreamed we could become.

In the gospel story Mark is showing us that this common human dependence on others is true even of Jesus. He is also suggesting something else, that we ourselves have a role here: to be fully himself, Jesus needs us, our faith and our belief and our love. He needs our commitment to him. Without those things he weakens, just as we would do. Thanks to Mark we have seen it happen.

Even Jesus cannot do it all alone. It was true then and is true now. This is what St. Teresa means in her famous prayer, when she says that Jesus has no hands but ours, no eyes and ears but ours, no way of acting in the world except through us. So now, today, Jesus needs us; he needs this church; he needs all his churches, of every kind and denomination.

If we walk away, the roof will collapse; grass and weeds will grow here in the nave; there will be nothing we could call a church, but an empty shell. We have that power. We can close our hearts and minds to the transcendent and amazing presence of God.

If we do, that holy presence will weaken and wilt, though it will not fail. Jesus' life and resurrection tell us that no matter how hard we try we cannot kill the divine force that lives at the center of the universe and at the center of each of us. It will always be there. But we can momentarily weaken it, by rejecting it.

In the second passage we hear of the twelve disciples, people just like us, who find themselves amazingly empowered to do miracles of a kind that normally Jesus alone can do. They can heal the sick and drive out demons.

What explains their new power? I do not think it is magic. I think it is the fact that Jesus, the human presence of God on earth, has perfect faith in them. He has confidence that they can do what he asks. They know this, and they can do it.

So here is the question for us today. Can we recognize Jesus' faith in us? Yes, that is right: not our faith in him, but his in us. Can we see and believe that the God of the universe knows us, trusts us, has faith in our goodness and our competence? Can we? If we can, what will it mean? What will we be able to do?

We learn from Mark that to be completely who he is Jesus needs us and our faith in him, and that to be completely who we are we need him and his faith in us. But there is another dimension to all this: we need not only Jesus; we need each other. No one can be a Christian alone.

Just think of the people in this room. We might have met as fellow passengers on a bus, say in Chicago or South Bend. What would we have been to each other? Strangers. We would not have been gathered in Christ's name, and he would not have been present to us. But instead we meet here, in this church, as others meet in other churches across the world, where we commit together to a life of trust and love.

This commitment is what enables Christ to have his full existence here, in this space; and his full existence here is in turn what enables each of us, and us together, to have our full existence too.

AMEN

Questions

1. Have you ever had the experience of moving away and coming home? How does your experience compare with what happens to Jesus in this story?

2. Have you ever had the experience of finding that when you are with another particular person, or with a certain group of people, you can

act and speak and feel more effectively, more powerfully, more gracefully than you could do by yourself? You might find yourself saying, "With him or her or them I always seem to be more fully myself."

Have you ever had the opposite experience, that when you are with a certain person or group you feel inept and ineffective and just not capable of acting and thinking and feeling fully as yourself?

How can you explain these experiences? How do you compare them with the experiences of Jesus and the disciples in this gospel passage?

3. Is this passage telling us what to look for in a community or friendship we are thinking of joining? In a church?

4. If Jesus is the Son of God, one would expect him to need nothing. But it is clear that he needs us: he needs us to be his hands, he needs us to build and maintain his church, he needs us to carry out his hopes for the world. What does this fact mean, about him and about us?

5. If you were to write a prayer after reading and thinking about this passage, what would it be?

2

"Many of His Disciples Turned Back"

In this passage from the Gospel of John, Jesus talks to his disciples about "eating his flesh and drinking his blood." This horrifies some of the disciples, who leave his company. Peter and the rest of the twelve, however, remain with him.

As you read this story you might imagine that you are one of the disciples to whom he is speaking. What would you say or do if Jesus suddenly started talking this way? What would it be like for you to leave him? To stay with him (then and now)?

The Gospel of John 6:56–69

"Those who eat my flesh and drink my blood abide in me, and I in them. Just as the living Father sent me, and I live because of the Father, so whoever eats me will live because of me. This is the bread that came down from heaven, not like that which your ancestors ate, and they died. But the one who eats this bread will live forever." He said these things while he was teaching in the synagogue at Capernaum.

When many of his disciples heard it, they said, "This teaching is difficult; who can accept it?" But Jesus, being aware that his disciples were complaining about it, said to them, "Does this offend you? Then what if you were to see the Son of Man ascending to where he was before? It is the spirit that gives life; the flesh is useless. The words that I have spoken to you are spirit and life. But among you there are some who do not believe."

For Jesus knew from the first who were the ones that did not believe, and who was the one that would betray him. And he said, "For this reason I have told you that no one can come to me unless it is granted by the Father." Because of this many of his disciples turned back and no longer went about with him.

So Jesus asked the twelve, "Do you also wish to go away?" Simon Peter answered him, "Lord, to whom can we go? You have the words of eternal life. We have come to believe and know that you are the Holy One of God."

The Church of the Mediator, August 23, 2009

May the words of my mouth and the meditations of my heart be always acceptable in thy sight, O Lord, my strength and my redeemer.

In the passage from John we just heard, Jesus talks about himself as a kind of food, saying things like this: *"Those who eat my flesh and drink my blood abide in me and I in them." "Whoever eats me will live because of me." "The one who eats this bread will live forever."*

This talk about eating flesh and drinking blood certainly must have sounded strange, even horrific, to the disciples. To us it may not be quite so weird, because we know about the Eucharist and can understand that Jesus is talking at least in part about that sacrament. But the disciples knew nothing of the Eucharist. They knew only that Jesus was talking in a way that sounded cannibalistic and was certainly in violation of the taboos of religious law.

So they say, understandably enough, "This teaching is difficult; who can accept it?" When Jesus does not explain to them what he means, some leave: "Many of his disciples turned back and no longer went about with him."

Today it is these people I want to think about, those who turned back. Can we imagine what they were feeling when they did this?

They had known Jesus personally; they had left their jobs and families to be with him; they had walked with him, watched him do miracles, heard him preach; but when they are told about eating flesh and drinking blood, they just cannot make head or tail of it; they are horrified by it, and they leave. When they leave, the last words Jesus said to them are ringing in their ears: "*No one can come to me unless it is granted by the Father.*"

How do you suppose they felt? Confused, I am sure, and in doubt about themselves and what they were doing. But maybe they also felt a kind of relief that they had escaped the clutches of a cult that was based on some craziness about eating flesh and drinking blood. After all, they did not know what was going to happen in Jesus' life, his death and resurrection. When they got home to their houses and families, they may have felt they were returning to a kind of sanity, back to the way things ought to be.

But I imagine that this condition, if it existed, did not last very long. They had known life with Jesus after all, this burning flame of love and power. They had been transformed by him. Life without him must have seemed dull and empty by comparison. They go back to their work, but what does it mean? What does *anything* mean in a world without God?

Surely the people who turned back felt that life had been drained of meaning. Perhaps they now asked themselves in a deeper way, "Why did we leave him? There was something about him that transformed each of us, transformed life itself. Life with him was full of meaning, full of joy. That was life at its most real, and intense and true."

There seem to be two logical possibilities here. One of them is that it was their own fault that they left. They had some inner defect that kept them from having the kind of real faith that Peter had, or perhaps they just weren't good enough to be one of Jesus' followers. This would, of course, make them feel terrible.

The other is that they were right: they left not out of weakness but for a good reason, which is that what Jesus was saying was truly frightening and made no sense. How could they stay, then, even to be with him? We know that there have been cults in our own time that promised life but delivered death, and this has always been so. To protect ourselves against them we need the power of reason and of truth. And what Jesus was saying did not make sense, it really did not—certainly not to those people.

Here is the problem that they faced, and that we face too. It has to do with the very nature of faith itself.

Faith is not reason. What faith commits us to *never* "makes sense" in the usual way. What we believe about Jesus, our Christian faith, will not "make sense" to someone outside of the church. That Jesus was both God and a human being, that he died a criminal's death, that he was raised from the dead and promises us eternal life: we believe these things, but to other people they will make no sense at all, and the idea of his crucifixion may horrify them. Have you ever tried to use reasoning to persuade a skeptic of the truth of what we believe? I have, and in my experience at least, it cannot be done.

It is not just our faith that makes no sense to the rational mind, but all faith. So far as I know, no religion really makes sense outside of the world it creates. Think of the Greek and Roman belief in many gods, for example, or an animist belief that the world was created by a Great Otter out of a universal sand pile, or the doctrines of the Mormon church, or the diverse gods of the Hindus. Lots of the people who believe in these things are of course sincere and good, but if we are honest with ourselves we know that we could not believe in any of them. They just don't make sense.

So we have to expect that the essential stories and doctrines of a religion, including our own, will not make sense of the usual kind to someone outside the community, or even to the side of the believer—the side of us—that functions by practical reason or abstract logic: the side on which we depend so heavily to make our way through the world.

But that is in fact part of the point: it is both the burden and the promise of faith that it does not "make sense" in the usual way.

We might think of it this way: faith is a way of knowing when to trust what cannot be explained in purely rational terms.

I think here of St. Augustine's *Confessions*. This is the autobiography of a very smart, intellectual man, who was led when young into Manichaeism, a sort of mystical and heretical version of Christianity. He liked it for certain intellectual reasons; yet he struggled with it too, also intellectually, testing its doctrines with philosophic thinking. He wanted to use his immensely powerful mind to understand God and himself.

The turning point in his story comes when he says, not in these words but in effect, "I knew, without knowing how I knew, that God was within me." (This is a theme especially of Book Seven.) He was grounding himself on a truth that he recognized deep within himself but could not explain to his rational neighbor or to the rational side of himself. Like any intellectual, Augustine had always prided himself on knowing how he knew; but now he finds himself saying, "I knew without knowing how I knew."

That is the posture of faith.

It is the posture of Peter. I think that none of what Jesus is saying about eating flesh and drinking blood makes any sense to him either, not a particle of sense. How could it? I think he certainly could not have explained it. But he cannot leave Jesus. Why not?

For Peter it is not a question of "making sense" or not; it is a question of deep internal identity--Jesus' identity and his own--and of equally deep commitment, a matter of love and trust. Wherever Jesus is taking him Peter will go, even if it involves talk about eating flesh and drinking blood, even if it means crucifixion, even if it means unimaginable dangers. He knows, without knowing how he knows, that he can and should build his life upon this person he loves.

Our faculty of reason is a good thing, and we need the protection it affords us. It can help us find our way to God. But we also need our organ of faith, and to live by its promptings. Not to do that would be a kind of death, even insanity. Yet our organ of faith prompts us, like Peter, to take an immense risk, a risk against what our sober, secular self is saying.

How can we do that? How can we know that the call we hear, the prompting of faith, is right? It is dangerous if we fail, either way: if we are deluded into following a false prophet, a false god, we may end up crazy—maybe drinking Kool-Aid laced with cyanide in a Central American jungle, as actually happened a few years ago. Faith and love and trust can be misplaced. But if we fail to follow a true prophet, a true god, we end our days in emptiness and loneliness and despair, without faith and love and trust at all.

So how do we face this deep uncertainty?

It is a little like the decision to get married, or to form any similar bond of commitment with another person. In such a relationship, we give ourselves to another, for our whole lives. This could of course be disastrous if we prove to be wrong. The marriage or friendship can turn out to be sick, like a sick prophet. This has happened to people we know; perhaps it has happened to us. But it would also be disastrous if we turned our backs on love and trust, and never really tried to live from the center of our hearts with another loving soul.

So how can we know what to do? I think only out of the kind of inner knowledge that Augustine had: "We know without knowing how we know." We ground our lives on knowledge of ourselves and the other person. It does not make sense of one kind, but in another way it is the only thing in the world that does make sense. If we are to be complete people who live fully, we must act on what we know without knowing how we know it.

Look at Peter. Peter knew Jesus. That is what he depended on: his knowledge of Jesus and his experience of himself when he was with him. We know Jesus too, and we know each other. Do we turn our backs on him? On each other? We have the life of our church, which has done much to form us. Do we turn our backs on that?

Or, to think of the baptism we are about to celebrate, do we turn our backs on Colin Arnold, who will be baptized this morning? I happened to meet him just before church, and he is a lovely little boy, full of life and trust and love. Shall we turn our backs on him? No: it is unthinkable.

In refusing to turn our backs on the church, on each other, on Colin, we are refusing to turn our backs on Jesus, for he is in each of us. We build on our faith; we build lives for ourselves; and we build a church in which we can live, and in which Colin will be able to grow up, learning how to trust himself and others. He will be learning the essence of love and trust and faith.

We know, without knowing how we know.

AMEN

Questions

1. Have you ever had the experience of knowing something to be true without knowing how you knew it? What did this knowledge lead you to do, to become?

2. Have you ever had the opposite experience, of refusing to commit yourself to something because it did not make sense to your reasoning mind even though your inner self supported it? What did this decision lead you to do, to become?

3. How do you judge from your present situation in life what you did on these occasions? Were you right both times, wrong both times, or right once and wrong once?

4. Think now about how you would try to explain to a skeptic why you go to church. Do you think you could make sense of what you are doing in a way that he or she could appreciate and understand? Why or why not? If you could not, does this mean the skeptic is right and you are wrong?

3

Trust and Fear

This passage from Mark has three parts: Jesus' prediction of his death and resurrection, his response to the disciples' argument with each other about who was the greatest, and his telling them to welcome a child he takes in his arms and places among them. What relationship do you suppose exists among these three elements of the story? Why are they put together in this way?

As I suggested earlier, it might be a good idea to pay attention to your own responses, to the questions and uncertainties that arise as you read. You might write them down.

You may sense that there is something wrong, askew, in the relation between Jesus and his disciples. What is it, do you think?

The Gospel of Mark 9:30–37

They went on from there and passed through Galilee. He did not want anyone to know it; for he was teaching his disciples, saying to them, "The Son of Man is to be betrayed into human hands, and they will kill him, and three days after being killed, he will rise again." But they did not understand what he was saying and were afraid to ask him.

Then they came to Capernaum; and when he was in the house he asked them, "What were you arguing about on the way?" But they were silent, for on the way they had argued with one another about who was the greatest. He sat down, called the twelve, and said to them, "Whoever wants to be first must be last of all and servant of all." Then he took a little child and put it among them; and taking it in his arms, he said to them, "Whoever welcomes one such child in my name welcomes me, and whoever welcomes me welcomes not me but the one who sent me."

The Church of the Mediator, September 20, 2009

May the words of my mouth and the meditations of my heart be always acceptable in thy sight, O Lord, my strength and my redeemer.

Today's Gospel seems to have an odd structure, falling into three parts.

In the first part Jesus is teaching his disciples about what is going to happen to him: his betrayal, death, and resurrection. Not surprisingly, the disciples do not understand what he is saying. How could they? What Jesus says, especially about rising from the dead, is so far outside their prior experience of human life that of course they have trouble grasping it. To begin to understand it they will have to live with what Jesus is saying, over and over, as we all have to live with any new and perplexing truth—as we have had to live in fact with old and perplexing truths, like the truth of the Resurrection. So it makes good sense that the disciples did not understand Jesus.

But what comes next is troubling: we are told they were afraid to ask Jesus what he meant. Why were they afraid? We shall come back to this.

The second part of the passage has no obvious connection with the first. Jesus has seen his friends arguing on the road, and he asks them, "*What were you arguing about on the way?*" A natural question, I think, for someone in Jesus' position: perhaps he thinks he can clarify matters, or even resolve the dispute. But the disciples do not answer. They remain silent, presumably because they are afraid to admit that they were arguing about who was the greatest. This is their second expression of fear.

Let us think for a moment about the argument itself: "Who is the greatest?" What a subject! Can we today imagine two surgeons, or lawyers, or professors, or movie stars, or football players arguing about which of them is the greatest? It seems very childish, and it may not happen very often in such an explicit way.

But in another way it happens all the time. If we look through the surface of what people are saying to what is really going on—to the tone of voice, body language, assumed right to speak, power to interrupt, claim of right to be heard, and so forth—I think we can often see an intense struggle over dominance and prestige, whether we are in the schoolyard or the operating room. People may not often *claim* to be the best, but they often spend a lot of energy trying to *prove* that they are the best. Whatever form it takes it is not very pretty.

The bad news is that we share the impulse ourselves. The ambition to be number one, to be the best—to be king of the mountain, to be the big enchilada—is deep in our nature. We are constantly asking how we rank, on one scale or another. Who is bigger, stronger, smarter, better looking, richer?

This impulse is in fact a root of serious sin, in all of us: envy and pride, anger and resentment, hatred and contempt.

What does Jesus do about the fact that his disciples are caught up in such an argument? Without being told, he understands what they have been doing, and he corrects them with a paradox: "*Whoever wants to be first must be last of all and servant of all.*"

What does he mean by this? Does he mean that if you are humble and low now, hungry and dressed in old clothes, you will able to swagger around in heaven, dressed in silks and lording it over others? Of course not. Jesus is completely opposed to our thinking that we are better than others, or our wanting to be better than others, in whatever form we do it.

I think he is really saying that "being first," in the sense in which the disciples, and we, normally think of it, is ultimately a self-destructive goal, empty and vain. "Being last" is somehow the right place for his followers, and it will not make them "first" in the eyes of the world.

It is the right place for Jesus himself. He is the least and last of all, a man who will be tortured to death as a common criminal. But in this very act his love shines out with a brilliance and power that transforms the world. He is truly last and truly first.

In the third section, Jesus takes a little child and puts it among them, taking it into his own arms, and says, "*Whoever welcomes one such child in my name welcomes me, and whoever welcomes me welcomes not me but the one who sent me.*"

On many scales of value and power a child is the least and the last. He or she has no power, no money, no capacity to fight and kill, no savings, no prestige at all. Children are all in the present, alive, full of promise, full of the future, full of hope. They are open to the future. They have a bone-deep capacity for trust: trust in their parents, trust in life itself. Think how a child's face looks as she raises it to her parent's face, in joy and hope and pleasure, knowing she is loved.

What Jesus says to his disciples, and to us, is beautiful. He does not say, "Be *like* a child," which we may not be able to do. He says, in effect, "*Welcome* the child," which, if we have any of the Spirit within us, we should be able to imagine and to do.

Think what it means to us to welcome a child. We ourselves are changed: our faces soften, our eyes brighten, our defenses and fears slip away. I am told that in every culture people looking at a new baby become dewy-eyed in exactly the same way. It is a human universal.

This is the change that Jesus wants to see in his disciples: he wants to see them drop their fears, open their hearts, and become capable of trust. He wants them to be ready to give of themselves to protect this vulnerable being before them. This is what Jesus means when he says that when we welcome a child we are welcoming Jesus, and when we welcome Jesus we are welcoming the Father.

How do these three passages fit together? I think the common theme is fear. In the beginning the disciples were afraid to ask Jesus what he meant when he told them what was going to happen to him; later they were afraid to admit that they were quarreling about who was the greatest. Notice that in both cases their fear barred them from Jesus himself. They could not ask Jesus what he meant, and in this way they prevented themselves from learning from him. They tried to keep secret what they were arguing about, and in this way they isolated themselves from Jesus' correction, teaching, and love.

In the passage about welcoming the child Jesus is also talking about fear, telling the disciples to discover what it is like to take the risk of opening themselves to him by opening themselves to a child they love, without fear.

Fear isolates; it is a box that fences off the world. It fences off love and discovery and growth. Fear comes from lack of trust. So Jesus is saying something like this, both to his friends and to us: "Welcome the one who can trust. Become one who can trust. Become one who can welcome a child, who can welcome me, who can welcome the Father. Fear not."

How does this passage about fear and trust speak to us in this church, especially at the beginning of the season of stewardship, which is now upon us?

Directly and plainly, I think. The theme of the passage is: put your fears behind you and open yourselves to trust, open yourselves to your own capacity for trust. Jesus is speaking directly to us at this moment, for it is fear that makes us reluctant to give of ourselves—just as it is fear that makes us want to "be first."

If we can welcome the child, in others and ourselves, maybe we can be transformed, from being people of fear to being people of trust. Maybe we can flower into those for whom first and last, greatest and least, will have no meaning. We won't be afraid of losing; we won't be afraid of life. We shall be welcoming Jesus and the Father who sent him.

The Stewardship Committee has decided on a theme for this season: "The Body of Christ, the Bread of Heaven." The idea is that yeast, which represents our loving support of the church, in all its forms, is what gives life to that bread, that body.

As I thought about this I thought about something from my own experience. So what follows is a little personal. Most of you know my wife Mary, of course, but you may not know that she has been making bread, two loaves at a time, once or twice a week, every week, ever since we were married. She has been doing this always from the same sourdough starter. I think she has made at least four thousand loaves from that starter during our marriage, maybe five thousand loaves.

The starter still has all vitality and force that it ever had. Giving did not make it weaker; it kept it healthy. The same is true of the loving and caring heart with which she kneaded and baked the bread for her family.

You and I, all of us really, have "starters" of our own—loving hearts—from which we too have made loaves of spiritual bread, maybe innumerable loaves, which we have given away. We have done this without diminishing or losing the starter at all. It is always there, still the same, a source of infinite life and love. It is not smaller or weaker because it is giving, but stronger and healthier for all its acts of trust and love. In fact, just like the bread starter, the human heart needs to give of itself or it will become sour and useless.

Jesus tells us that we are not to be afraid of life, not to be afraid of giving of ourselves, not to worry about who is first and last, who is the greatest, but to be present in the world as sources of welcoming love, present as those who welcome the child, welcome Jesus, welcome the Father. When we do that, we shall be transformed from people of fear to people of trust.

May we welcome the children who trust and need us.

May we become the body of Christ, the bread of heaven.

AMEN

Questions

1. Where do you find yourself in this story? Among those mystified by the Resurrection, among those quarreling about their own importance, among those to whom Jesus shows the child? You might ask yourself: what does each of those events mean to me?

2. Each of us has fears that inhibit and hobble us. Can you identify some of the fears that have kept you from acting freely and lovingly and strongly in the world? Can you imagine what it would be like to be free of those fears? Can you hear Jesus promising to help you be free of them?

3. The opposite of fear is not bravery or rashness, nor is it the sort of denial by which we so often keep our fears hidden from our conscious selves: it is trust. What would it be like to trust life, to trust the world, as Jesus would have us do? What would it be like to trust Jesus himself? Think here of your own experiences of trusting, being trusted.

4. Jesus wants us to be welcoming to the children we meet. This is good for them and for us. Perhaps he also wants us to be welcoming to the child within us, to give that child a place and standing in our thoughts and feelings and decisions. Is this something that you have ever done? That you could imagine doing? What would it be like?

Here someone might say, "I have spent my whole life growing up, and I don't want to revert to being a child." How would you answer such a person, or such a voice within yourself?

5. If you were to make a prayer in response to what Jesus says here, what would it be?

4

The Widow's Mite

As you read this famous story about the scribes and the poor widow, ask yourself in which of these characters you find yourself represented. Are you a scribe? The widow? One of the disciples? Imagine yourself as deeply as you can into the situation of one of those people. How do you think Jesus is speaking you in the role you have chosen? How is he speaking to all of us, now?

The Gospel of Mark 12:38–44

As he taught, he said, "Beware of the scribes, who like to walk around in long robes, and to be greeted with respect in the marketplaces, and to have the best seats in the synagogues and places of honor at banquets! They devour widows' houses and for the sake of appearance say long prayers. They will receive the greater condemnation."

He sat down opposite the treasury, and watched the crowd putting money into the treasury. Many rich people put in large sums. A poor widow came and put in two small copper coins, which are worth a penny.

Then he called his disciples and said to them, "Truly I tell you, this poor widow has put in more than all those who are contributing to the treasury. For all of them have contributed out of their abundance; but she out of her poverty has put in everything she had, all she had to live on."

ST. ANDREW'S CHURCH, NOVEMBER 8, 2009

May the words of my mouth and the meditations of my heart be always acceptable in thy sight, O Lord, my strength and my redeemer.

THE GOSPEL READING WE just heard consists of two passages: Jesus' warning to beware of the scribes and the story of the widow's gift, a gift that was tiny in purely economic terms, immense in spiritual terms. It is a hard passage for us, I think.

"*Beware of the scribes,*" says Jesus. These people walk around in front of the Temple in their elegant clothes and are greeted with respect by the people they meet. Their value and status are constantly confirmed on all sides. Jesus criticizes them strongly, but in doing so I do not think he is making a final judgment on the state of their individual souls—which may have been tortured with guilt and remorse, for all we know—so much as drawing attention to the kind of life they lead, to the human possibility they represent.

They are stereotypes, and as such they present a remarkably effective image of what today we might call the "successful" or "prosperous" or "important" person—the kind of person that, at least in some secret part of ourselves, almost all of us would like to be or become. To take a heavily clichéd example, think of men at a country club, all wearing similar uniforms, whether their fine business suits or their casual clothes from L.L. Bean or their expensive athletic garb. They are constantly confirming each other's value in their greetings and their talk, yet at the same time they are establishing a hierarchy among themselves.

Some of these men are important people, like the scribes, who do not greet others but are greeted by them, who do not seek out others but are sought out, who do not listen to others but are listened to. Their jokes are laughed at, their styles of dress and speech imitated. Others, less powerful, do the greeting, the smiling, the respecting. In this world everyone wants to be in the position of power, like the scribes.

Of course it is awfully easy to say such things about country clubbers if, like me, you have never belonged to such a group. But the truth is that exactly the same thing goes on in other contexts, say, just for instance, in a department or school at the University of Michigan, where some people are greeted, some greet; some are listened to, others listen; some are imitated, others imitate. In fact, the scribes are very much like a bunch of professors.

The truth is that everyone, including us, seems to want to be part of the "in-crowd," to be in a position of power, just like the scribes. When there is a banquet, everyone wants to sit at the head table. I think this would even be true at a clergy conference. In our various worlds and in our own ways, we are too much like the scribes, of whom Jesus tells his followers, and us, to beware.

Why does Jesus tell us to beware of them? The main reason is to warn us of the danger that we ourselves might become even more completely like the scribes than we already are. Jesus is right to warn us about this. Every step in this direction is a fall into sin. The motives that Jesus wants us to live by are directly opposed to the motives at work in the scribes, and in us as scribes: Jesus wants us to show love, not contempt, for the poor and weak; humility, not pride, in our sense of ourselves; attention to heavenly things, not earthly things; attunement to the life of the Spirit, which seeks to save us and transform our lives, not submission to an empty desire for power and prestige, which brings death to the soul.

The scribes also do real, sometimes terrible, damage to other people and cover it up with hypocritical pretensions. They devour the houses of widows, but say long prayers in public to create the appearance of piety and decency. In this way they benefit from an economic and social system that exploits other people for their benefit, and then promote an ideology that hides that reality.

So Jesus is saying to his followers, and to us, beware the scribes lest you become more fully like them and do the kind of damage they do, to themselves and others.

Sometimes it is hard to see the danger they represent. The scribes seem like nice people, and they may be genuinely unaware of the exploitation in which they engage or from which they benefit, just as we ourselves tend to be. For them, as for us, it is easy to say, "I work hard for my income. I am paid the going rate. I am not a gouger or a cheat. I am entitled to what I have. I am in fact generous with my wealth," without for one minute thinking of what it costs other people that we live as we do. But if the scribes succeed in dominating the world, they do damage not only to themselves but to those they dominate. This is of course true of us as well.

We are all implicated in a social and economic system in which some people benefit, sometimes hugely, at the expense of others. In some respects we exploit; in some we are the exploited. There are disputes about the precise figures, but it is clear that a tiny percentage of the people in our country own a hugely disproportionate percentage of the wealth. From the newspaper we know that annual salaries, and bonuses, of tens of millions of dollars are the lot of some, while hard times, often real poverty, sometimes desperate poverty, are the lot of many others—around the world, the lot of billions of people.

This not good for anyone. So Jesus rightly says, "*Beware of the scribes.*"

In the second part of the reading Jesus and his friends are watching people make gifts to the Temple treasury. A series of rich people give large sums, then a widow puts in two copper coins, worth only a penny. Jesus says that she has put in more than all the others, because while they gave out of their abundance, she gave all she had.

There is a large point here, a point of economic theory. Jesus is saying that the widow's penny is worth more than a rich man's gift of any amount, at least so long as it is short of all he has. Her gift of a penny is thus worth more than a gift of a hundred million dollars from a billionaire.

This is not what an economist or university president would say, nor what we would normally say. But Jesus has his own kind of economics, a vision with radical consequences. For Jesus recognizes that a dollar, or a copper penny, in the hands of someone who really needs it is worth much, much more than a dollar or a penny in the hands of one who has lots of them. This means that for him the richest society is not the one with the greatest total wealth but the one in which wealth is shared most equally.

For us this means something very troubling: that we should look at our own bank accounts in a different way, recognizing that they seriously misstate value. As the accounts get bigger the dollars gradually become less valuable to us and to the world; as the dollars are put in the hands of people poorer than we are, they become more valuable. What Jesus is saying is that to distribute wealth to those who do not have it is actually to create wealth. This is not, to put it mildly, the usual way economists or politicians think. But it is true.

In these two passages Jesus is proposing a complete, almost unimaginable transformation of the way we live our lives. In the passage about the scribes, he says that a fundamental aspect of our social psychology needs to be changed: we should no longer seek to be powerful ourselves, no longer curry favor with the powerful, no longer desire the best seat at the banquet, no longer want to have power or prestige in any form. This sounds good. But how can we do it? How can we give these things up? The desire for them seems built into our nature.

In the passage about the widow, Jesus challenges a central feature of our economic thinking, telling us that we are to reimagine the dollar, not as a fungible unit of currency, of the same value in anyone's hands, but as a unit whose value depends entirely upon the wealth or poverty of the one who is holding it. For him it is only in an economically equal world that the dollars are equal, and only in an equal world that we can be truly prosperous: only in a world in which the equal value of every person is recognized, not only in our long and public prayers, but in the way we live our lives. How are we possibly to live on these terms? The whole idea of money and bank accounts, of property and its accumulation, of mine and thine, seems to make it impossible even to imagine.

What are we to do? Of course I have no easy solution to this problem. The gospel brings us a challenge to the soul, and asks that we live with it seriously and eagerly. At the very least we should approach the issue prayerfully.

What should our prayer be? Perhaps something like this. We should ask for the grace of forgiveness, for our conscious and unconscious entanglement and participation in the world of the scribes; for the grace of enlightenment and guidance, in using our resources of time and money, especially for the benefit of others; for the grace of wisdom, in shaping a course of action; and for the grace of strength, in carrying it out; and, in all of this, for the grace of a deep change in our hearts that will help us follow Jesus in loving and caring for those who suffer.

AMEN

Questions

1. Are you ever eager to be thought important or powerful in the eyes of others, eager to be thought virtuous and good? Happy to be part of an in-group? Pleased with your status in the world, and not particularly interested in thinking about whether you really deserve it or what it costs other people that you have it?

Can you imagine not being like the scribes in these ways? What would that be like?

2. If you in fact benefit from a social and economic system you believe to be unjust, what would it mean to fully recognize that fact? How would you live and think and feel differently?

3. Think of the value Jesus places on the widow's two coppers and ask: are there places or moments in your life where you recognize that the value of money is not a constant, but goes down rapidly the more money a person has and rises rapidly the less money a person has? Are there times when you see money as a moral fact in the lives of others and yourself?

What would it mean to see, fully see, the difference between, say, five dollars to you and what we would call "the same amount" to one of the children climbing the garbage dumps in Manila, or going hungry in America? Does that difference entail a moral imperative to give and give until the value of a dollar to every person is the same? What limit, if any, do you think Jesus would put on that imperative?

4. Bring this line of thought to your own church, to both the Budget Committee and the Outreach Committee. What should it mean in practical terms?

5

The Temptation of Jesus

As you read this story about temptation, slow down and think about temptations in your own life and how you succeed or fail in resisting them. Maybe make a written list of temptations to which you have succumbed, another list of temptations you have successfully resisted. Why did you succumb to one set of temptations, and how did you resist the other?

How does this passage speak to you, as a person familiar with the experience of temptation?

The Gospel of Luke 4:1–13

Jesus, full of the Holy Spirit, returned from the Jordan and was led by the Spirit in the wilderness, where for forty days he was tempted by the devil. He ate nothing at all during those days, and when they were over, he was famished. The devil said to him, "If you are the Son of God, command this stone to become a loaf of bread."

Jesus answered him, "It is written, 'One does not live by bread alone.'"

Then the devil led him up and showed him in an instant all the kingdoms of the world. And the devil said to him, "To you I will give their glory and all this authority; for it has been given over to me, and I give it to anyone I please. If you, then, will worship me, it will all be yours."

Jesus answered him, "It is written, 'Worship the Lord your God, and serve only him.'"

Then the devil took him to Jerusalem, and placed him on the pinnacle of the temple, saying to him, "If you are the Son of God, throw yourself down from here, for it is written, 'He will command his angels concerning you, to protect you,' and 'On their hands they will bear you up, so that you will not dash your foot against a stone.'"

Jesus answered him, "It is said, 'Do not put the Lord your God to the test.'"

When the devil had finished every test, he departed from him until an opportune time.

The Church of the Mediator, February 21, 2010

May the words of my mouth and the meditations of my heart be always acceptable in thy sight, O Lord, my strength and my redeemer.

THE STORY WE JUST heard from Luke, about the Temptation of Jesus, is very familiar, but it is also a little odd: a bit like a fairy tale, somewhat schematic and removed from life. What can it mean to us?

One perhaps surprising thing to keep in mind, to begin with, is that the experience of temptation is in the end a positive one for Jesus. His time in the desert and his testing by the devil give him new knowledge and confidence. We see this in the very next passage in Luke's Gospel, when Jesus goes to the synagogue in Nazareth and declares that he is the Messiah foreseen by Isaiah. Jesus has new power. He is on his way. Surely his temptation has something to do with this. We should remember this when we think of temptations in our own lives, that they may be ways of making us better than we would have been without them.

Another preliminary thought: we are now at the beginning of Lent, the penitential season that is expected in some way to mirror Jesus' experience of temptation. A question to keep in mind as we think about this passage is: what can this story of temptation mean for us at the beginning of Lent?

During this season we are asked, like Jesus, to give up our usual habits of life, which absorb so much of our energy, and attend instead to the most important things, to eternal things. We are to break through the surface of life, and ourselves, and face what is deepest within us and in the world.

This is an inherently solitary activity, as Jesus shows: we can encourage each other, but each of us must go into his or her own desert and discover the truth that is there. It is possible that for us this truth will take the form of a temptation, a temptation by the devil, and we shall have to resist it as best we can. But we should also know that for us, as for Jesus, this might turn out to be a good thing, not a bad one.

The hope of Lent is that by the time Easter comes we, like Jesus, will be more fully who we are meant to be; that we can participate in that great moment, deeply and joyfully; and that we can carry our transformed selves into the life that awaits us after Easter, in what our liturgical calendar calls ordinary time.

This makes sense. But how are we to do these things? What help can we find in this story?

In thinking about how to read this passage I found very helpful something I read in George Lindbeck's book *The Nature of Doctrine*: just as it is our capacity to learn a human language that separates us from other animals, it is our learning of another language, "the language that speaks of Christ," that begins in us the process of becoming what St. Paul in one of his letters calls "a new creation" (Lindbeck, p. 62).

The first point, about language distinguishing us from animals, makes immediate sense. Language is the medium through which our intelligence works, through which we build human community, and through which we claim meaning for our lives. Animals have feelings, but they don't have language of a full kind. I think it is right that this distinguishes us from them.

The second idea is much harder, but also true: in addition to our natural language, say English or Spanish, we have another language to learn, "the language that speaks of Christ," and as we learn it and internalize it, each of us starts to become a different kind of human being, living in a different world.

This sounded puzzling to me at first, but then I recognized that we in this church have all already learned some of the language that speaks of Christ. Think how different our lives would be, for example, if we had never been exposed to that language. We would probably just be living out of our own wishes and desires, with no sense of meaning in life of the kind we have come to love: no Christmas, no Lent, no Easter, no church, no God. Life would be just one thing after another, without shape or significance. We might be good people, but our lives would lack the shape and meaning they have now.

So we have already used "the language that speaks of Christ" to organize our lives. It gives us a different sense of the nature of the world and the meaning of life, of our sorrows and joys, of our successes and failures. We already live in a new world, one in which we are beginning in a new way to know who we are, where we come from, and where we are going. But our work is incomplete. Our task is to continue bringing this language into our souls throughout our lives.

What happens if we try to bring the story of the Temptation into our souls, if we try to make it part of the way we experience the world and act within it?

Here I want to look at three parts of the story. The first is the beginning, where we are told that Jesus was full of the Holy Spirit and that the Spirit led him into the desert. Suppose we were to take just that much into ourselves, and make it a part of us. The word for what we would be doing is prayer: not prayer in the sense of asking for something, but prayer as a way of opening our hearts and spirits to the Holy Spirit, letting that presence come into our souls, where it may move and grow and change us—where it may lead us into something new. That is what Jesus did.

We know from Jesus' example that when we do feel the Spirit within us, we are to follow where it leads, even to a waterless desert. We are to trust it, as Jesus trusted it. So the first stage of bringing the passage within is *trust*, especially *trusting the Spirit*.

The next step in Jesus' experience, we are told, is his fasting for forty days. We know that we cannot go without food for as long as that, but is there something like it that we *can* do in this season of Lent that might bring what Jesus is doing deeper into our hearts and souls?

Probably like many of you, I think of giving up something: ice cream or wine or reading detective stories or watching basketball on TV. But this is not the kind of fasting that this story suggests. No: the idea is that I should give up all those things, and many more. Not because they are bad. I don't even have to stop doing them. For what I am really to give up is not the things themselves, but what they mean to me, and the meaning of all these things is the same: I am the center of the world, and what should shape my life is my own set of wishes and satisfactions.

But to give up my sense that I am the center is more than I can do, except maybe very briefly. It is a little as though I am asked by this passage to go on a forty-day silent retreat, focusing only on what God is telling me, deep in my heart, and never experiencing distraction. I cannot seem to do that. Probably you cannot either. But it may be a good thing to see more fully what we are called to do, even if we cannot do it.

Perhaps the second stage of bringing the story into our souls is a kind of *perceiving*, especially *perceiving what we are called to do*. For us, unlike Jesus, there is an additional dimension to this stage: perceiving that we cannot do it, perceiving that we need help even to try to resist our sense that we are the center of the world.

When we turn to the third stage of the process, the temptations themselves, we see that Jesus' response is in each case to quote a relevant passage of scripture:

> "*One does not live by bread alone.*"
>
> "*Worship the Lord your God, and serve only him.*"
>
> "*Do not put the Lord your God to the test.*"

To us, who are trying to figure out how we can internalize the language of God, what Jesus does here is amazingly helpful. He is actually showing us how the language of God can be made part of the self and put to work in human life. This is what he is doing. He is showing us how he made his religious language part of his very self, as we should also do. He uses it to resist the devil. How can we use it?

Can we bring this passage to the temptations of our own lives, especially the temptations that parallel those of Jesus? Most of us are tempted, for example, by the desire for material things. We wish we could turn stones into bread, or what will buy bread, namely, money. No wonder: we have deep within us the desire for acquisition, and it is constantly stimulated by the barrage of advertisements we see on TV or in the newspaper. Our lives thus have literal temptations, the temptations of material possessions and the money that can buy them. When faced with these temptations, what can we say to ourselves?

Jesus shows us: "*One does not live by bread alone.*"

Suppose we are tempted by power and prestige, the sense of ego importance that comes from a position of authority, in our company or town or church. We are all tempted to try to become important. If we do this we will be making idols of ourselves, as Jesus is also invited to do. If we are tempted this way, what can we say?

Jesus shows us: "*Worship the Lord your God, and serve only him.*"

Or suppose we are tempted in a more subtle way, by the desire to make God do what we want, in order to prove that he exists, has power, and cares for us. It may be a surprising thought, but we do this, I think, whenever we demand of God that he heal a sick person or get us a job or bring peace to the world or just solve some other problem we have, for we are impliedly threatening him with abandonment if he does not do these things. "If you don't do this, I won't believe in you." When we find ourselves doing that, what can we say?

Jesus shows us: "*Do not put the Lord your God to the test.*"

So perhaps the third stage of bringing the language of God into the heart is a kind of *learning how to use*, especially *learning how to use that language*: learning how to use what we read and hear, how to make it our own as we respond to our temptations. It is of course not enough just to quote this phrase, or any of the things Jesus said, as if it were a magic formula. If what we say is going to stand up to the devil, it must come from a place deep within us. It is our task to bring this language into that place.

Trusting the Spirit, perceiving what we are called to do and become, and learning how to use the language of God: these are all ways of learning "the language that speaks of Christ" and bringing it within ourselves to become a new creation.

One final point. Once Jesus has repudiated the temptations, he turns from what seems like a magical world, a world of fantasies and false promises, to an actual life, a life like our own, one that will have to be lived through day by day, hour by hour, with particular people, in particular places, at particular moments. This life is full of difficulty and uncertainty and irritation and failure, for him as well as for us. In Jesus' case it will ultimately mean abandonment, betrayal, and crucifixion. For us it will mean failure, times of isolation, and suffering.

Perhaps we are asked by the gospel to internalize this movement too, to bring it within us: Jesus' movement from fantasy to reality. If we could do that, we would stop daydreaming so much. We would become alert to our own false hopes and empty values, to our own desires for instant and impossible gratification, to our own grandiosities. Remembering Jesus, we might then turn to the new life we have been given and accept it joyfully, with all its limits and difficulties. This, too, would be part of becoming a new creation.

In trying to do this we shall not be alone, even though we are certain to fail to do it perfectly. For in making his return to ordinary life, Jesus is showing us that he, and the Spirit, are not off in some land beyond the clouds, but here, with us, in the life they have chosen to share with us.

This is where God is, in our lives: here with you and me, now, today. In the Hebrew word that we know from the Christmas story, *Emmanuel*: God is with us.

AMEN

Questions

1. I have suggested that there are parallels in our own lives to the temptations Jesus experienced in the desert. As you think about your own experience, do you find that these parallels are real? Are there other temptations you also regularly face? Thinking of them one by one, are there ways you can imagine using the "language that talks about Christ" to respond to them?

2. Have the temptations in your life ultimately been good experiences, as they were for Jesus, or bad ones? Who is it that determined which they were? Is it possible that they were good experiences, even if you succumbed to them?

3. As you think about the way the language that speaks of Christ can be brought into your life, into your soul, do you find that the stages I suggest—trusting the Spirit, perceiving a call, and learning how to use the language of God—apply to your experience, or for you does this process work in different stages?

6

Amos and the Good Samaritan

This time we have two readings, one from Amos, one from Luke. As you read them ask what connection can sensibly be drawn between these two texts, written in such different times and circumstances, and addressed to such different audiences. Why do you suppose the lectionary includes both of them? Why in fact does it ever include readings from what we call the Old Testament?

In particular, as you read the Amos passage imagine that you are he. Would you speak as he does? If so, when and why? If not, why not?

As you read the story of the Good Samaritan, let me suggest that you take the time to read it three times slowly, imagining yourself first as the injured man, then as one of the priests, then as the Samaritan. What do these events mean to you in each role?

Then imagine yourself as the innkeeper. What do you suppose all this means to him?

The Book of Amos 7:7-17

This is what he showed me: the Lord was standing beside a wall built with a plumb line, with a plumb line in his hand. And the Lord said to me, "Amos, what do you see?" And I said, "A plumb line."

Then the Lord said, "See, I am setting a plumb line in the midst of my people Israel; I will never again pass them by; the high places of Isaac shall be made desolate, and the sanctuaries of Israel shall be laid waste, and I will rise against the house of Jeroboam with the sword."

Then Amaziah, the priest of Bethel, sent to King Jeroboam of Israel, saying, "Amos has conspired against you in the very center of the house of Israel; the land is not able to bear all his words. For thus Amos has said, 'Jeroboam shall die by the sword, and Israel must go into exile away from his land.'" And Amaziah said to Amos, "O seer, go, flee away to the land of Judah, earn your bread there, and prophesy there; but never again prophesy at Bethel, for it is the king's sanctuary, and it is a temple of the kingdom."

Then Amos answered Amaziah, "I am no prophet, nor a prophet's son; but I am a herdsman, and a dresser of sycamore trees, and the Lord took me from following the flock, and the Lord said to me, 'Go, prophesy to my people Israel.'

"Now therefore hear the word of the Lord. You say, 'Do not prophesy against Israel, and do not preach against the house of Isaac.' Therefore thus says the Lord: 'Your wife shall become a prostitute in the city, and your sons and your daughters shall fall by the sword, and your land shall be parceled out by line; you yourself shall die in an unclean land, and Israel shall surely go into exile away from its land.'"

The Gospel of Luke 10:25–37

Just then a lawyer stood up to test Jesus. "Teacher," he said, "what must I do to inherit eternal life?"

He said to him, "What is written in the law? What do you read there?"

He answered, "You shall love the Lord your God with all your heart, and with all your soul, and with all your strength, and with all your mind; and your neighbor as yourself." And he said to him, "You have given the right answer; do this, and you will live." But wanting to justify himself, he asked Jesus, "And who is my neighbor?"

Jesus replied, "A man was going down from Jerusalem to Jericho, and fell into the hands of robbers, who stripped him, beat him, and went away, leaving him half dead. Now by chance a priest was going down that road;, and when he saw him, he passed by on the other side. So likewise a Levite, when he came to the place and saw him, passed by on the other side. But a Samaritan while traveling came near him; and when he saw him, he was moved with pity. He went to him and bandaged his wounds, having poured oil and wine on them. Then he put him on his own animal, brought him to an inn, and took care of him. The next day he took out two denarii, gave them to the innkeeper, and said, 'Take care of him; and when I come back, I will repay you whatever more you spend.'

"Which of these three, do you think, was a neighbor to the man who fell into the hands of the robbers?" He said, "The one who showed him mercy."

Jesus said to him, "Go and do likewise."

The Church of the Mediator, July 11, 2010

May the words of my mouth and the meditations of my heart be always acceptable in thy sight, O Lord, my strength and my redeemer.

I AM SURE IT is on all of our minds that this is our first day of worship in our new building. It is so bold and beautiful and spacious, such a great and generous achievement on the part of so many people, especially those who actually built it, with their hands, during a bitter winter. It represents an amazing amount of love and hope and labor. We should enjoy this wonderful moment to the full.

But what will this change mean? We are giving up a beloved space, modest and familiar, where many things of the greatest importance have happened: baptisms, funerals, weddings, our weekly Eucharist—all that is involved in our life together.

Now we are—well, where exactly are we? What life will we make here? What connection will it have to the world? These questions may make all of us a little anxious. Let us see what today's Scripture tells us about the kind of life God wants us to make here.

Our two readings offer two models of life, two ways of serving God and connecting to the world. The first is that of Amos, who was a prophet, traditionally the earliest of the prophets. He spoke for the Lord, saying a deeply unwelcome truth: that Israel was doomed, doomed because it disregarded fundamental justice. Israel failed to protect the most vulnerable members of its community: the poor, the widows, and the children. And Amos was right. Israel was doomed: not long after he spoke, the Assyrians came and took over the land.

Is Amos a model for us? Are we supposed to be prophets too, individually or as a parish? This is a truly hard question. Amos has deep insight into the purposes of Yahweh. He can see that God really wants his people to be just. Israel's injustice is a violation of the covenant God made with his people, and he is angry. This is the truth of God that Amos speaks in the face of all opposition. He burns with zeal for justice for the poor. Jesus did too.

We need people like that, in the church and in our country. We certainly need to hear the truth that our God wants us to live justly and mercifully and generously, to care for the poor and the helpless. We need to hear it when we are failing to do those things.

So: yes, we should be prophets?

But there are dangers in such a course. How do we know what God wants? Maybe we are preaching what we want, not what God wants. There is such a thing as a false prophet—Jesus warned his followers against them—and we do not want to be false prophets. Indeed, it may seem that in our world we have too many self-styled "prophets" already: people angrily declaring with certainty and self-righteousness what they take to be the will of God.

So: no, we should not be prophets?

But sometimes there is an evil that calls out to be named and resisted. Should we not do those things? If there have been false prophets, there have been true prophets too. Think of Martin Luther King or John the Baptist or Jesus himself. And a prophet need not be angry or condemnatory. Think of peaceful Quaker witnessing, for example.

What are we to do? Should we sometimes speak out clearly against the injustices of our world, striving to utter not our truth but God's truth? When should we do this? How do we know when we are truly called to do so, and how we ought to respond to that call?

I do not have any ready answer to these questions, but I do think Scripture is clearly telling us they are important. Perhaps they can best be taken to define a topic for prayer, for each of us, and for all of us together, as we shape our new life in this new space.

When we look at the Good Samaritan we see a very different kind of person from Amos, a different way of serving God, a different way of connecting to the world.

The story begins when a lawyer asks Jesus what he needs to do to inherit eternal life. Jesus asks him, "*What is written in the law?*"

The lawyer knows the right answer: you should love God and your neighbor. This is the core of Jesus' whole teaching. It is the heart of what he is telling us to do, in this new building and in our lives: to love God and our neighbor. That sentence could in fact be the cornerstone of our life together.

But what does it mean exactly? The lawyer wants to know the answer, and asks, "Who is my neighbor? Who is it that I am to love?" In response Jesus tells the famous story: a man beaten by robbers is lying beside the road; two priests pass right by, but a Samaritan, a social outcast, stops and cleans his wounds, takes him to an inn, and promises to pay his entire bill.

Jesus then asks the lawyer, "*Which of these three, do you think, was a neighbor to the man who fell into the hands of the robbers?*" The answer is of course obvious: the Samaritan.

Notice that Jesus is no longer addressing the lawyer's question—"who is my neighbor?"—though it is clear that he thinks the answer is everyone, even a stranger lying injured by the road. Rather, here Jesus is addressing a different issue: what is it like to love our neighbor, to be a good neighbor, in the way Jesus wants us to?

This love is what the Samaritan represents. Part of it is of course that he physically tends to the man and his wounds. But perhaps it is equally important how he does these things. For, as I imagine it anyway, the Samaritan is not anxious or irritated or driven by a sense of duty, but completely natural and centered. He is not afraid or self-conscious, but deeply and directly present as a mind and soul to the injured man, and to his situation. He is not trying to solve all the problems of the world, but to meet the need before him.

If I were to find an injured person by the road, I hope I would be like that, but I am afraid I would not. I am afraid I would be anxious, self-conscious, embarrassed, undone by the sight of the wounds and my own sense of helplessness. I would probably call the police or an ambulance on my cell phone, and maybe hang around long enough to be sure they got there. Then I would feel good about myself, for being a Good Samaritan.

But I would be wrong. The Samaritan does not look upon the injured man as a difficulty to be dealt with efficiently, nor as a source of embarrassment.

No: he sees the injured person as a whole person, as a child of God; he responds to him fully, with generosity and care. He dresses the wounds himself, slowly and patiently, with his own hands; he leaves the highway to take the man to an inn, where he can be cared for; he assumes responsibility for all the expenses of his stay. In this way he brings the injured man wholly into his imagination and his heart. The injured man is a call to him, a call from God.

I imagine that the Samaritan demonstrates this remarkable way of being all the time: when he speaks with a child in the grocery store, when he sits next to someone at church, when he responds to a question from a man in the street, when he sits with his dying parent or brother or child.

His art is the art of being present, wholly present to the realities of the world and to the experience and needs of others. That is his way of loving his neighbor and, in doing so, loving God. This way of being is in fact a manifestation of God, alive and at work within him.

What are these passages telling us as we begin our new life in this building?

I think they are presenting us with this question. Is it sometimes our duty to be a bold prophet like Amos—like John, like Jesus? This is a dangerous thing to do, practically and morally, dangerous for ourselves and others. It is surely a task we should undertake only after deep prayer and with some fear and trembling, lest we find ourselves projecting our own evil onto others so that we may safely condemn it.

But Amos and Jesus seem to be telling us that it is sometimes our duty to be a prophet. If so, we have to find our own way of doing it, one that would be a good way of reaching out from our church to the world. That is our task, and it is not small. It ought to be a continual part of our thinking and praying.

The readings also offer us the model of the Samaritan. Here I think we are being told that we should imitate him throughout our lives, trying to practice his art—the art of being wholly present to others in love—as much as we possibly can. This is his way of connecting to the world, and we should try to make it ours as well.

The trouble is that the standard is too high for us: to be like the Samaritan is to be like Jesus himself, which we cannot do. But Jesus knows we will fail, and we know that he will forgive and support us if we turn to him with open and contrite hearts. So we are to aspire faithfully to the ideal the Samaritan represents.

I have spoken of the prophet and the Samaritan as contrasting figures, but maybe they can be brought a bit closer together as we imagine our future in this church.

Would it not be a kind of prophecy if we could live as the Samaritan does, out of love for God and our neighbor? Would it not be an act of love worthy of the Samaritan if we could truly say to the world what God wants us to say? Both would be ways of connecting to the world, ways of reaching out to others and inviting them to join us in the life we, with God's great help, are creating here.

AMEN

Questions

1. Think for a moment about the role of the Old Testament prophet. Does anyone perform such a function today, in the church or out of it? Should this kind of prophetic voice be a part of our religious life? When? If the answer is, when we are called, the next question is: how do we know when we are called?

2. The lawyer who asked Jesus how he could inherit eternal life actually knew the answer: he could quote to Jesus the two great com-

mandments that he, Jesus, had identified. So why does he ask the question? And when Jesus tells him he has answered correctly, why does he ask the next question, "Who is my neighbor?" What is bothering him? What does he want from Jesus?

3. Think about the parable as addressed specifically to the young lawyer, and ask: where does it leave him at the end? What has Jesus done to him, done for him?

4. In understanding the story itself it may be useful to know that if a priest touched a dead body he had to go through an extensive rite of purification. This may help explain why the priests turn aside. Are there any modern parallels to this sense that the touch of another might be polluting? What should we do about them?

5. It may also be useful to notice the fact that the ethnic and religious identity of the injured man is never made plain. He was probably a Jew, since he was going from Jerusalem to Jericho, but maybe not. Maybe he was a Samaritan. What does Jesus' silence on this matter mean? It would have been important to all the actors in the story. Is Jesus saying, especially to the young lawyer, that it ought not to matter at all?

6. The Samaritan not only rescues the man and brings him to the inn, where he dresses his wounds and feeds him. He pays his bill for several days, and tells the innkeeper to charge anything else to his account. This feels like more than moral duty, more even than generosity would require. Maybe it is the enactment of perfect, even excessive generosity. He does more than anyone would. What is the significance of that fact?

7. If you were to compose a prayer after reading these passages, what would it be?

7

The Woman in the Synagogue

In this story a woman, who has been badly crippled for eighteen years, comes to a synagogue where Jesus is teaching on the Sabbath. Jesus calls her to him and heals her. Indignant at this, the leader of the synagogue protests—but somewhat oddly, for he does not attack Jesus for healing on the Sabbath, but attacks the woman for coming to be healed on that day.

Let me suggest that you read this three times slowly, first imagining that you are the woman, then that you are Jesus, then that you are the leader of the synagogue. Imagine each role as fully as you can: think of the space in which the events take place, the temperature and quality of the light, what you can see and hear and taste and touch and smell, what you hope and fear, what you expect. Put yourself into the role as fully as you can. Which role fits you most readily?

To do this will require a substantial piece of time, but I think it will be worth it.

The Gospel of Luke 13:10–17

Now he was teaching in one of the synagogues on the Sabbath. And just then there appeared a woman with a spirit that had crippled her for eighteen years. She was bent over and was quite unable to stand up straight.

When Jesus saw her, he called her over and said, "Woman, you are set free from your ailment." When he laid his hands on her, immediately she stood up straight and began praising God.

But the leader of the synagogue, indignant because Jesus had cured on the Sabbath, kept saying to the crowd, "There are six days on which work ought to be done; come on those days and be cured, and not on the Sabbath day."

But the Lord answered him and said, "You hypocrites! Does not each of you on the Sabbath untie his ox or his donkey from the manger, and lead it away to give it water? And ought not this woman, a daughter of Abraham whom Satan bound for eighteen long years, be set free from this bondage on the Sabbath day?"

When he said this, all his opponents were put to shame; and the entire crowd was rejoicing at all the wonderful things that he was doing.

The Church of the Mediator, August 22, 2010

May the words of my mouth and the meditations of my heart be always acceptable in thy sight, O Lord, my strength and my redeemer.

W E HAVE JUST HEARD a complex story. Let's work our way into it by thinking of each of the characters in turn.

We can start with the woman. She has been so severely beset by disease that she has not been able to stand up straight for eighteen years. She comes into the synagogue—which may not be a building, but a place of assembly in the open air—where Jesus is teaching.

We do not know why she came before Jesus. She does not ask him to cure her, nor does she touch his robe or sandals. I imagine that she just came to hear him teach, or to be near him, maybe not thinking about her infirmity at all.

Have you ever had that feeling, that there was someone so full of love and goodness and strength that you just want to be near him or her? Not because of anything he or she would do for you, but just because the nearness itself is such a blessing? This is how I think of the woman. She is not in Jesus' presence to ask for anything. She does not know what he will do, but she trusts him completely. Whatever he does will be right and good.

In the midst of his teaching, Jesus sees the woman, calls her to him, and declares, *"Woman, you are set free from your ailment."* He touches her, and she stands up straight, completely cured. For her this is not just an abstract "miracle," an act meant to demonstrate Jesus' power, but the transformation of her whole life. She is freed in a way she could never have imagined.

Notice how she responds. She praises God. She does not thank Jesus; she praises God. She is a model of faith.

It is at this point that the leader of the synagogue speaks out. He is not the Pharisee or scribe we might expect, but just a lay leader, the equivalent perhaps of an Episcopal senior warden. He does not attack Jesus for healing—he probably does not dare—but attacks the woman for coming to be healed.

"There are six days on which work ought to be done," he says; "come on those days and be cured, and not on the Sabbath day." This is the wrong time and place.

Think what this verbal assault means to the woman. At the moment of the greatest blessing in her life she is falsely accused of a kind of selfish seeking that violates a religious law. Just when she is most completely aware of the presence and working of God, full of praise and openness, the leader tries to turn the opinion of the whole crowd against her as wrongdoer. What an injury at such a time! What a way to respond to the miracle of generosity and healing to which they have all been exposed!

We should ask why he behaves in this injurious and unkind way. Can we imagine ourselves into his shoes?

I can. All I need to do is remember when I was a teacher and think how I would respond to any interference with the way my class was going—which was very defensively, and not nicely. I think the leader may be in a somewhat similar situation. Maybe he even called the people together to hear this exciting new teacher. In this case, it is his show and must go as he planned. If it goes well, people will be admiring and grateful; if it goes badly, people will criticize him. Or maybe he felt from the beginning that Jesus was a kind of invader of his terrain, forced on him by circumstance.

In either case, he feels threatened and angry because his ego is so completely at stake in his capacity to control events. All he can see is that his plans and authority have been interfered with, and he is angry, scornful, and rude. What he cannot see is that what has happened before his eyes is the presence of God at work in the world.

We all know enough about plans of our own to see something of ourselves in this man. Suppose a person performing some miraculous act of God interrupted the wedding we had been planning for months or interfered with a fiftieth birthday party in our honor or even disrupted a church service in this very room: might we not want to send the offending person away, saying that this is not the time or place for such things?

This passage is asking us to pray that our self-centeredness, our anxiety, and our need to control may not blind us to the presence and action of God before us: the God who is always present within us and around us, always acting, if we only have eyes to see and ears to hear.

The third person in this story is of course Jesus. He responds to the leader not to in order defend himself but to protect the woman against this attack. He speaks entirely in terms of her situation:

> *"You hypocrites! Does not each of you on the Sabbath untie his ox or his donkey from the manger and lead it away to give it water? And ought not this woman, a daughter of Abraham whom Satan bound for eighteen long years, be set free from this bondage on the Sabbath day?"*

Notice that in describing the work that people ought to feel free to do on the Sabbath, Jesus does not talk, as he sometimes does, about an obvious emergency, say an animal falling into a well, but about simply taking an ox or donkey from the manger, where it has been feeding, and leading it to get water to drink. What trumps the Sabbath here, then, is not a matter of physical life and death, but common decency and humanity: giving animals water when they are thirsty. That is what Jesus is doing too: offering this woman water, the water of life—and, in doing so, offering that water as well to the crowd, to the leader, and to us.

It is often said that we should try to lead our lives in imitation of Christ. What would it mean if we were to take what Jesus does in this story as a model for our lives?

Jesus is busy teaching in the synagogue, perhaps focusing on the scripture that he is interpreting and on his audience, looking for quizzical looks or signs of boredom, trying to articulate the truth, but then something else happens: he sees a woman come in who cannot stand up; he stops what he is doing and calls to her, touches her, cures her. He responds to a call.

Suppose we are similarly absorbed in some activity we think important when suddenly there appears before us a woman who needs our help. Will we even notice? Her presence is a call: a call to attend, to listen, to respond with love and readiness to the need before us, whether her need is a medical emergency, a sorrow, or a sense of exclusion or helplessness—whatever it is. In the story Jesus hears that call, and we are to do so too. We are to drop the activity that is an extension of our ego, just put it aside, and attend to what is real in the person before us.

Just as the leader teaches us by his negative example that we are not to be blind to the presence and activity of God, Jesus is teaching us by his positive example that we are not to be blind to our own opportunities to do God's work.

The opportunities for doing this work are not rare or mysterious. Maybe we experience a dozen of them every day, mostly without noticing: in the hardware store, at our workplace, on the sidewalk, even in coffee hour after church—moments when we are called on to respond to another with compassion and love.

We may not be able to cure physical ailments, but there are lots of suffering people to whom we can respond, if we have eyes to see them: a frightened child, a grieving man who is afraid to show his feelings, a person who needs five dollars for a sandwich, a stranger in church who needs a welcoming look and a smile. All these are God's calls to us if we can see them.

In thinking of this story—of all three people: the woman, the leader, and Jesus—I was reminded of a statement I once read by a well-known theologian. Speaking of his own failure to live out the gospel in his life, he said somewhat ruefully, "I live most of my life as if God did not exist."

That is true of the leader of the synagogue, who lives as if God did not exist at the very moment when God is visible before him. It is true of us too, at moments in our own lives when God's call is before us, unseen and unheard. It is of course not true of Jesus. What would it be like always to be deeply aware of the presence of God, within others and within ourselves?

Let us think again about the afflicted woman. Remember that when she comes before Jesus she does not ask for anything; she certainly does not complain or plead or demand; she is not anxious; she stands simply in his company, experiencing the blessing of his presence. She is silent, and full of trust. She knows how to be in the presence of God.

She is fulfilling the command that is reported in the Psalms: "Be still and know that I am God."

May God give us grace to do the same.

AMEN

Questions

1. As you think of the woman in the synagogue, can you imagine how you yourself might ask for help from God? What kind of help would you ask for? How would you ask? In particular, can you imagine simply presenting yourself in trust to God, as the woman does, without any plea, complaint, or argument? It might be worth trying to do that the next time you turn to God in need.

2. As you think of the leader of the synagogue, can you find parallels in your own experience to what he feels and says and does? Sometimes we have the feeling that an event is somehow our show, whether it is a class or a party or a meeting of some sort, say a political meeting or a religious service. When we feel ourselves in that position we want everything to go according to our script and are angry when things work out differently. Have you ever been in such a situation, with such feelings? What did you do about what you felt to be a disruption? What do you now wish you had done?

3. As you think of Jesus responding to a call–a call never given voice by anyone but a call nonetheless–can you find parallels in your own life? Have you ever felt such a call? What did you do about it? What do you now wish you had done about it?

8

Lazarus and Dives

Let me suggest that this time you follow the same practice you used in reading the passage about the woman in the synagogue, namely, that you read this story about the rich man and the poor man by going through it twice, once from the point of view of Lazarus, once from the point of view of the rich man, in each case imagining yourself as fully as possible into the shoes of the person you have chosen.

Then ask our familiar questions. Where are you in this story? What is Jesus saying to you in telling it?

The Gospel of Luke 16:19–31

"There was a rich man who was dressed in purple and fine linen and who feasted sumptuously every day. And at his gate lay a poor man named Lazarus, covered with sores, who longed to satisfy his hunger with what fell from the rich man's table; even the dogs would come and lick his sores. The poor man died and was carried away by the angels to be with Abraham.

"The rich man also died and was buried. In Hades, where he was being tormented, he looked up and saw Abraham far away with Lazarus by his side. He called out, 'Father Abraham, have mercy on me, and send Lazarus to dip the tip of his finger in water and cool my tongue; for I am in agony in these flames.'

"But Abraham said, 'Child, remember that during your lifetime you received your good things, and Lazarus in like manner evil things; but now he is comforted here, and you are in agony. Besides all this, between you and us a great chasm has been fixed, so that those who might want to pass from here to you cannot do so, and no one can cross from there to us.'

"He said, 'Then, father, I beg you to send him to my father's house—for I have five brothers—that he may warn them, so that they will not also come into this place of torment.'

"Abraham replied, 'They have Moses and the prophets; they should listen to them.' He said, 'No, father Abraham; but if someone goes to them from the dead, they will repent.'

"He said to him, 'If they do not listen to Moses and the prophets, neither will they be convinced even if someone rises from the dead.'"

The Church of the Mediator, September 26, 2010

May the words of my mouth and the meditations of my heart be always acceptable in thy sight, O Lord, my strength and my redeemer.

Today we have the famous story of Lazarus and the rich man, who is traditionally called Dives (pronounced Dye-Vees), the Latin word for "rich man."

Dives is rich and enjoys the benefits of his wealth: fine linens, good feasting every day, and a handsome house. Lazarus, at his gate, is utterly poor, weak, and sick. The dogs lick his sores. When Dives dies, he goes to the place of eternal punishment, while Lazarus goes to the bosom of Abraham. That is the story.

Dives is not sadistic. He does not take pleasure in the suffering of Lazarus, nor does he triumph over him; he is just takes no notice of him at all. Even though in one sense he sees Lazarus every single day, in another sense he never sees him at all. He is simply blind and deaf to the human suffering before him.

This blindness continues after his death: even in hell, Dives does not see Lazarus as the person whose suffering he could so easily have relieved; he does not feel guilt or shame or repentance at his own failure to help. Instead, he sees Lazarus simply as a messenger boy. He never recognizes the humanity of Lazarus.

Jesus, of course, recognizes the full humanity of every person, and he wants us to do that too.

Why does Dives not see that Lazarus is a person? Maybe he is just so wrapped up in a program of self-gratification that he can see nothing else. That is probably part of it, and it is certainly familiar to all of us from our own experience of self-involvement.

But maybe there is something deeper than that, something I see hinted at in the great difficulty I myself have in responding properly to a homeless person I meet on the street. I am ashamed of the fact, but there is a part of me that does not want to be connected to the Lazarus before me. I feel embarrassed and helpless.

I think what I am feeling is a complex fear. Part of it is the fear that if I recognize the humanity of Lazarus I will have to recognize as well the duty to help him. After all, in our baptismal covenant, which we shall repeat later today, we promise, with God's help, to respect the dignity of every person, and that means giving help where necessary. I am afraid what that might mean.

But I think there is another, even deeper element in the fear I describe, namely, that to recognize the humanity of Lazarus is to recognize that his lot might be my lot. After all, we are all ultimately vulnerable to the same losses, disturbances, illnesses, and sufferings that we see before us in Lazarus. We could end up like him, without a home, without resources.

Even if we do not become homeless, every one of us, no matter how rich and powerful, will certainly die, often in pain and sometimes in despair. We can all be reduced to pleading lumps of flesh by disease or disaster. Likewise, any one of us can succumb to mental illness and lose his or her sense of identity and connection with the world.

The truth is that we might end up like Lazarus, a possibility so awful that we erase him from our minds.

Even worse: I think there is a sense in which we are like Lazarus now. He represents a side of ourselves we want to hide. So when I see Lazarus, I see a secret side of myself, one that is like him vulnerable, disturbed, dependent, weak, pleading for support. Lazarus is like a mirror, showing me an aspect of myself I try to hide. I see myself in the face of Lazarus, and I turn away.

What is true of me may be true of Dives. I imagine him as a competent and successful man, maybe not a lawyer or hedge fund operator but someone like that, who takes great satisfaction in his power, in his control, in his capacity to make things come out his way. I think that he does not see Lazarus for all the reasons I have suggested: he is preoccupied with his program of self-gratification; he does not want to face the obligation that such recognition would entail; Lazarus's lot may be his lot; and he does not want to face the truth that there is an inner Lazarus within him—that he is Lazarus.

In his blindness to Lazarus, Dives is blind to himself. He is denying not only the humanity of Lazarus, but his own humanity. This is what we do too.

The story tells us that when he dies Dives finds himself suffering in hell. Abraham says this is perfectly fair: the law and the prophets told Dives clearly that he had an obligation to help the poor and the suffering and he did not do it. So he cannot complain about the consequence of eternal fire.

What Abraham says makes a kind of sense, but I think it is not what Jesus would say. For one thing, Jesus knows that a person like Dives, whose life is governed by needs and fears and compulsions that are as deep as those I have mentioned, cannot really be reached and corrected by the mere statement of a moral rule, even if it is enforced by a threat of hell.

Think of someone you know who seems caught up in an empty and unfulfilling life: pursuing money with abandon, as if happiness lay there; or acting as a slave to some kind of addiction; or smothering his children with what he thinks of as love or punishing them severely "for their own good." Imagine trying to tell such a person what you see him doing, where you see him going, in the hope that he might change.

We have all done this. Do we succeed? Not usually. Where a person's deepest selfishness and sins are at stake he or she won't usually respond to advice, even loving advice, and that is true not only of others but of us as well. We may read the law and prophets, but we do not absorb them. We need something else, infinitely more powerful and loving. What we need, what Dives needs, is Jesus himself.

Notice that Abraham does not tell us why a loving God would ever send anyone to eternal torment. I think that God does not in fact send us to hell: we send ourselves there. Dives has cut himself off from humanity, and in doing that he has cut himself off from God. This means that he was actually in hell when he was alive, even though he thought the opposite, that he was a great success, enjoying the good life.

We too may have had a similar experience of deep emptiness beneath a surface of success and satisfaction.

Now think of Dives, and of us, from the point of view of God. God does not want Dives to go to hell. He loves him, as he loves us all. But how can he reach Dives? The law and the prophets did not do the job. So what is God to do?

Maybe God says something like this.: "I do have one last hope: if my Son comes and lives with you, and shows you what I want you to be, and if he dies for you, and comes back from the dead, a transformed being, to call you to life—to life that really is life—then, maybe, you will turn from the empty existence you are choosing for yourself and embrace the way of life and of love."

Like Dives, what we need is a complete transformation of the self, a turning inside out and upside down, a reorientation of every part of our being. A statement of moral rules or even divine commands cannot achieve that kind of change. To make that kind of transformation possible, Jesus comes to live with us, to love us, to die for us, and to return to us, as the Resurrected Christ.

True sin is not really a set of bad acts or omissions; it is a state of isolation from love, a repudiation of love, of our own capacities for love, and it can be reached only by love.

This gospel tells us, then, not only why Dives denied the humanity of Lazarus, but, much more important, what it is that Jesus wants to change, in him and us and the world, by living among us, dying for us, and returning to life again, victorious over death.

I have said that we are all Dives. That is true, but we should not forget Lazarus. As I said, we are all Lazarus too.

Lazarus is loved by Abraham, not because he is good but because he is a suffering human being. He may in fact be lazy and dishonest; he may be mentally ill. But he suffers, and Abraham loves him.

The part of us that is like Lazarus is weak, suffering, afraid to act, without any value in the eyes of others or ourselves; without entitlement to anything; raw, chaotic, suffering, confused. It is this part that Jesus so easily loves. He does not like the Dives in us, the proud and controlling part, the part that is afraid and embarrassed at the sight of Lazarus. He wants us to change. His way of helping us do that is by loving us: by loving the person within us who has been twisted into the form of a Dives; and also by loving the other person within us, the Lazarus, the one that Dives disowns, disregards, despises. If we can allow ourselves to recognize the Lazarus within, we may be able to hear the saving words of Jesus speaking within our hearts: we are loved, we are loved, we are loved.

It is not the bright, confident, competent Dives within us who will save us, but the wounded, weak, and despised Lazarus. Maybe the next time we see Lazarus on the street we can see the Jesus in him, and he can see the Jesus in us.

Today we celebrate the baptism of two boys, Hartley and Declan, who have been made members of the family of Christ. Let us pray that God will give them the grace to grow straight and tall, out of the center of their souls, into boys and men who can always recognize, respect, and respond to the humanity of everyone they meet.

AMEN

Questions

1. What would it actually mean, mean in practice, to recognize fully the humanity of Lazarus, of Dives, of ourselves?

A question like that has no easy or formulaic answer. It must be lived with, day by day; we must work out our responses as we are confronted again and again with Lazarus, on the streets and in our hearts, with Dives, in his splendid house and in our hearts, and with ourselves. How can we do this and do it well?

That is the question the gospel puts to us, and helps us face: not by giving formulas or rules, but by engaging us, over and over, with the different stories and the tensions between them, always in the presence of Jesus.

2. One way into our question is to ask another: can we recognize that hidden part of ourselves that is like Lazarus? If so, will that help us recognize the humanity of the real Lazarus we meet on the street?

3. The gospel is asking us to do the same thing with Dives. Can we recognize that part of ourselves that is like Dives? Does that help us recognize the full humanity of a real Dives?

4. Now imagine that Jesus is present before you, looking at you, seeing your full humanity, who you really are. What does he see?

9

The Pharisee and the Tax Collector

In the passage that follows a clear contrast is drawn between the Pharisee, who adheres to the law and does what he can to maintain the religion of his people, and the tax collector, who works for the occupying Roman forces to extort money from the people of Israel. Perhaps in the process he makes what he would call a very good living.

When you read it, ask which of these is most like you. What do you think Jesus is saying to you in this passage?

The Gospel of Luke 18:9–14

He also told this parable to some who trusted in themselves that they were righteous and regarded others with contempt.

"Two men went up to the temple to pray, one a Pharisee and the other a tax collector. The Pharisee, standing by himself, was praying thus, 'God, I thank you that I am not like other people: thieves, rogues, adulterers, or even like this tax collector. I fast twice a week; I give a tenth of all my income.'

"But the tax collector, standing far off, would not even look up to heaven, but was beating his breast and saying, 'God, be merciful to me, a sinner!'

"I tell you, this man went down to his home justified rather than the other; for all who exalt themselves will be humbled, but all who humble themselves will be exalted."

The Church of the Mediator, October 24, 2010

May the words of my mouth and the meditations of my heart be always acceptable in thy sight, O Lord, my strength and my redeemer.

In this passage Luke makes a point of telling us that the people to whom Jesus presented this parable were some "who trusted in themselves that they were righteous, and regarded others with contempt."

These people do two things: they *trust in their own righteousness* and *have contempt for others*. They are not as righteous as they think they are. We should keep these people very much in mind, because we are among them. The whole story is told to us, and is about us.

Jesus tells us that two men went to the Temple to pray. One man, a Pharisee, prays by thanking God "that he is not like other people: thieves, rogues, adulterers, or even this tax collector here." The tax collector prays by simply saying, "God, be merciful to me, a sinner!"

It is easy to see who is right here, and who is wrong. The Pharisee is a self-righteous prig, confident in his capacity to please God; the tax collector is a sinner and knows it, and he asks from his heart for mercy. Jesus tells us that it is the tax collector who goes home "justified" or righteous, not the Pharisee. We nod in agreement.

But notice: when we do this, we fall into a trap. We feel confidently superior to the Pharisee, but in fact we are being just like him: trusting that we are righteous, and holding him in contempt. The parable thus invites us to commit the very sin it represents, bringing it from the outside, in other people, to within us, where it can be seen and felt and maybe corrected.

I think we are not to condemn the Pharisee in this easy and superior way. We need to look at him as one of us, and at ourselves as one with him. What he is doing we all do, and we need to understand it.

Let us think some more about the Pharisee. For me one question is this: why does the tax collector, along with the rogues and adulterers, appear in his prayer in the first place? Why is he thinking about these people at all?

The Pharisee is in God's holy Temple, in a special way in the presence of God, but what he is thinking about is not God, or even himself really, but other people: his difference from them, in particular how he is superior to them. This is what he wants to thank God for. Why? What is he doing?

I think he is manifesting a universal human instinct, one we ourselves share, namely, to think of himself constantly in comparative terms. We do this whenever we ask the question, "How do I compare with him, or with her, or with them? How do I rank, or rate, compared to him or her?" Or more brutally, "Can I hold him in contempt? Or can he hold me in contempt?" We think this way whenever we find ourselves saying, "What a slob!" or "What a jerk!" or "I wish I was as handsome or rich or accomplished as he or she is."

This impulse is familiar to all of us from our experience of high school. Are you a member of the in-group, powerful and glowing with self-confidence? Or are you a reject, an outcast, a geek, with no friends but other geeks? Or somewhere in between? In any case, you are situated on a ladder of prestige and power, and you know it—a ladder that has no real relation to human excellence. Those at the top tend to be conceited, full of themselves; those at the bottom tend to be depressed and miserable. Not a pretty picture.

This disease, so prevalent in adolescence, does not magically disappear as we get older, but continues in very much the same form all through life: in economic affairs, in corporations and universities, in labor unions and political parties, even in churches. Human beings put themselves on ladders, or in pecking orders, and they desire to be at the top. We cannot help it. It is our nature.

When we do compare ourselves to others, we may, like the Pharisee, feel an improper sense of superiority in ourselves, and contempt for others. But it is also true that like the low-status kid in high school we may feel something very different, namely, an improper sense of inferiority in ourselves and a corresponding envy for others.

Think of what the tax collector might have said in his prayer if, like the Pharisee, he had been obsessed with comparing himself to others: "Look at that Pharisee over there, who keeps your law in every respect and leads a righteous life. He is successful and important. Why did you not make me like him? Why can I not be like him?"

Whether we look up or down, the essential vice is the same: constantly comparing ourselves to others, asking where we are on the ladder. One way leads to contempt, the other to envy, and both are bad. The contemptuous person has a false sense of superiority, the envious person an equally false sense of inferiority.

The price paid by both kinds of people, and by us in both modes, is huge: it is the avoidance of real experience.

Think of this in the context of prayer, as Jesus asks us to do. If we are thinking all the time about how we compare with others on the ladder of prestige and power, we are not thinking about who we actually are, about who God is, about what God wants of us, or about what we need to do or become. We become incapable of true joy, true grief, true gratitude, and true remorse. Our prayer never gets going because we never stand naked before God.

This habit of mind makes it impossible for us even to give proper thanks for our blessings, since we are distracted by something else, something ultimately false: a comparison between our blessings and the blessings of others. We become incapable of heartfelt thanksgiving, heartfelt praise, heartfelt prayer.

What makes it even crazier, more twisted and impossible, is that when it comes to our status in the eyes of God there is no ladder at all, or if there is we certainly do not know what it is. As I imagine it, in fact, God does not compare us to each other, but treats us as the unique being each of us is, offering us his constant love and forgiveness.

Who are we to say that one person is more righteous than another, more blessed, more in tune with the love and will of God? Yet we do it. We do it all the time: we do it as the Pharisee, assuming that we are better than the sinner; we do it as readers, assuming that we are better than the Pharisee. We even do it institutionally, thinking that we Episcopalians have the best church of all, the most righteous, much better than the Roman Catholics or the Methodists or the Baptists. And why? Because we have the Book of Common Prayer and they do not! Thank God we are not like them!

Here is the problem. The impulse I have been describing, to think of ourselves in constant comparison with others, seems to be built into us, deep in our genes. We share it with baboons and chickens and maybe toads and moths. How can we possibly counteract this seemingly irresistible force?

It is to help us do this that Jesus comes among us, teaching us over and over that in the eyes of God all men and women and children are equal; all are his children; all are equally and infinitely loved. Like the elder brother in the story of the prodigal son, who resented the fuss that was made when the renegade came home in disgrace and humiliation, we are told, "You have me with you always. Everything I have is yours." We need not envy, and we need not have contempt.

Jesus is helping us resist something deep within us, deep in our nature, something that is, as a scientist would say, the product of evolution itself, or, as we Christians would say, the result of the Fall of Man.

It is the task of the church that Jesus established, including the Church of the Mediator, to strive to create the kind of community Jesus talks about, where all are equal before God and humanity. Here we have a chance to be who we actually are, to present our bare souls to God and to each other, not to be ranked by power or wealth or sanctity, but to recognize each other, as God recognizes us, as persons within each of whom is an infinite piece of God. No envy, no contempt, but a shared life and a shared world, where we know that God loves each of us infinitely, and know, too, that this is literally the only thing that matters.

Imagine it: being free of the curse of thinking of ourselves constantly in comparative terms, ranking ourselves and others, feeling envy and contempt. Instead I will just be me and you will just be you, as we are, without pretense and without shame, in the presence of God. When we pray we will be able to be grateful for our actual blessings without comparing them to those of others, and wondering why they are not greater; we will be able to ask for help with our afflictions, without comparing them to those of others, and wondering why they are not less. When face to face with God, which we know is all the time, we will be just ourselves, just as we are, making the prayers we need to make. It sounds like heaven. It *is* heaven.

But in the real world we know that we cannot fully attain this condition, no matter how much we try. We will keep trying, but we shall always fail, in big ways and small. For the most part all we get is glimpses.

So when we stand before God we know how to begin our prayer: "Have mercy on me, a sinner."

There is one thing left. This is stewardship season. But that does not really change the subject at all. For what Jesus is telling us here is that in thinking about our gifts in support of the church—or, better, our return to God of a portion of God's gifts to us—we should be guided by the knowledge that, wherever we may be, we are constantly in the presence of God, in his Temple. In this place there should be no contempt, no pride, no envy, no self-inflation, no self-abasement, but joy, heartfelt joy, that we know that we are each of us, and all of us, infinitely loved.

If we act in that spirit we will do the right thing.

AMEN

Questions

1. Can you make a list of occasions on which you have said or felt something like "Thank God I am not like other people"? Can you make a list of the people about whom you have said or felt it?

If you are inclined to say you never say such a thing, consider your attitude towards people who are sick, suffering, or in the process of dying, people who are in trouble with the law or addicted to alcohol or drugs, people whose grades in high school were much worse than yours, people who are as a matter of their character disposed to be hostile or rude or cruel, or people of a radically different political persuasion from you.

2. Are there occasions when you find yourself wishing that you had what someone else has: more money, better looks, a healthier body, more power? Can you make a list of such occasions and such people?

You may be especially likely to have such feelings when you are certain that those other people do not deserve what they have. Envy is inherently small-minded and mean and hostile, depreciating both oneself and the other person, who is enjoying such undeserved blessings.

What do you do about these feelings? What might you do?

3. Can you imagine a life in which you did not constantly make such comparisons?

4. Suppose you try to look at your social world with God's eyes, recognizing that there are human criteria for thinking of human excellence and success, but also God's criteria. When you think of the people you have looked down on (in response to question 1) or looked up to with envy (in response to question 2), how do you think God would value them? I think it would be useful to ask this questions with specific people in mind.

5. I have suggested that as I imagine him God does not engage in comparisons. Do you think it may also be true that God does not care about quantities? Think of a single mother of modest means caring for a single damaged child with love and attention and courage. Is she living the life God wants us her to live? Is she doing so less than someone out in the public arena, leading a movement to eliminate poverty or bring about world peace?

10

The Annunciation to Joseph

A lot of attention has been paid over the years to the Annunciation to Mary, which is treated in the Gospel of Luke with care and evident love and has also been the subject of countless paintings. Today's reading gives us the opportunity to think about the Annunciation to Joseph, as I am calling it: the way his difficult situation is explained to him by an angel, and how he comes to think about it. As you read the passage ask yourself at each stage how you would feel if you were in his place.

The Gospel of Matthew 1:18–25

Now the birth of Jesus the Messiah took place in this way. When his mother Mary had been engaged to Joseph, but before they lived together, she was found to be with child from the Holy Spirit. Her husband Joseph, being a righteous man and unwilling to expose her to public disgrace, planned to dismiss her quietly.

But just when he had resolved to do this, an angel of the Lord appeared to him in a dream and said, "Joseph, son of David, do not be afraid to take Mary as your wife, for the child conceived in her is from the Holy Spirit. She will bear a son, and you are to name him Jesus, for he will save his people from their sins." All this took place to fulfill what had been spoken by the Lord through the prophet: "Look, the virgin shall conceive and bear a son, and they shall name him Emmanuel," which means, "God is with us."

When Joseph awoke from sleep, he did as the angel of the Lord commanded him; he took her as his wife, but had no marital relations with her until she had borne a son; and he named him Jesus.

St. Andrew's Church, December 19, 2010

May the words of my mouth and the meditations of my heart be always acceptable in thy sight, O Lord, my strength and my redeemer.

Today is the fourth Sunday in Advent, our season of waiting and repentance. It is the time for us to open our hearts to be present to God when he comes.

We are almost there, as we know from today's Gospel, which might have a name of its own: "The Annunciation to Joseph." Mary is pregnant with Jesus. The bodies of both mother and baby are fully engaged in the mysterious process, both physical and spiritual, that is repeated in every human gestation: the process that results in the emergence of a new person, a new soul, into the world.

As any parent can tell you, it is not only the baby who is newly born. For all those who love the new baby, he or she transforms the whole world beyond imagining. This tiny, weak, utterly dependent person creates a force field of love around him or her that none of us grown-ups can begin to match. Call it infant power.

This time it is Jesus who will be born, with infant power beyond anything we know. As he grows he will create a force field of love that will run throughout the universe, for all time. Indeed, he is alive now, in all of us here today, in this church, in our hearts. His life is the miracle of all miracles.

One way we have learned to talk about the amazing and mysterious force of life and love that we see in Jesus is to call him "the Son of God." It is natural for us to think this way, because we are used to it, but it is also highly perplexing, as you know if you have ever tried to explain to a skeptic the double nature of Jesus, let alone the mystery of the Virgin birth.

But any intellectual perplexity we may feel at this theological problem must be nothing compared to Joseph's existential perplexity, his agony, when he faces a drastic real-world problem: he is told that his betrothed wife is pregnant, and he knows for certain that he had nothing to do with it. How does he deal with this difficulty?

We don't know everything he does, of course. Matthew tells us simply that Mary "was found" to be pregnant. We don't hear anything about the conversations that must have taken place between Mary and Joseph. What did she say to him? What did he say to her? How did they talk to each other? It must certainly have been distressing in the extreme for both of them. Perhaps they even said things to each other that would later require forgiveness.

Since in Matthew's story there has been no annunciation to Mary, she cannot even say that her pregnancy is caused by the Holy Spirit. She is just as mystified as Joseph is. She must be deeply confused and afraid; he must be completely puzzled and hurt and angry.

Matthew does tell us that Joseph decides to break off the engagement. This is hardly surprising. To him her pregnancy proves her unfaithfulness. He may think that as a man of honor in an honor society he has no other choice. But he is much less severe than he might have been, as we learn when we are told that he decides to "dismiss her quietly" rather than "expose her to public disgrace."

The phrase "public disgrace" is actually a euphemism that masks the full truth, for in exposing Mary to public shame Joseph would have been accusing her of adultery, and the penalty for that under the law was death by stoning. This a dreadful punishment, but you can see how it comes about. Then, as now, sexual betrayal is likely to breed in the injured person deep hatred and the desire to destroy.

But Joseph does not want to injure Mary. Despite what he feels to be a terrible injury at her hands, he does not want to destroy her. He wants to preserve her. I think he still loves her—she is still the same person, the same Mary, after all—even if it seems impossible for him to keep her as his wife.

Perhaps this very experience is teaching him something that will be evident in Jesus too, perhaps even something that Joseph will teach Jesus: the sense that violence is never a solution.

It is important to see that if Joseph had decided to expose Mary, the result would not only have been her death, but the death of the unborn Jesus too. If Joseph had made that decision, our Savior would never have been born.

What this means is that God's whole plan for his son Jesus—for his birth, his life, his death, his resurrection, the redemption of the whole world—depended upon the unaided judgment and character of this one man. God trusted Joseph with everything.

Joseph proved worthy of this trust. His initial decision to preserve Mary's life was made on his own, without any help from an angel. It was his own love, his own goodness, his own rejection of violence, that led him to the decision that made possible the emergence of Jesus into the world.

Of course the story does not stop there. Unless things change, Jesus will be born as the illegitimate child of an unmarried woman, a despised and dangerous status in the world in which they live. So the angel comes to Joseph in a dream and tells him that "the child conceived in Mary is from the Holy Spirit" and that he should not be afraid to take her as his wife.

How does Joseph respond? He does not doubt the truth of what the angel says; indeed he does not doubt that it is an angel speaking to him, though I suppose he might have feared that it was some kind of demon. He does not even ask the angel to explain what on earth he means when he says that the child is "from the Holy Spirit," which is not exactly clear even to us. When he awakes, Joseph simply obeys.

Why? My own sense is that this is another manifestation of the depth of his love for Mary. It is true that she told him something he simply could not believe, that she was a pregnant virgin, but she is still the woman he loves above all women, the person he trusts above all people. He wants to believe her. He just can't do it.

So I think he is ready to hear something, anything, that will enable him to do what he wants most in the world to do, which is to keep her as his wife and to share his whole life with her. Whatever his "rational" mind is telling him, in another, deeper place he knows that she did not betray him, that she could not betray him. For him she is the embodiment of truth.

Let us now stand back a moment and ask what is at stake in this story, first for Jesus, then for us.

First, for Jesus. For him Joseph's first decision, not to expose Mary to public shame, was necessary to his being born at all; his second decision, to keep Mary as his wife, was also necessary, not for him to be born, but for him to grow up in a family grounded in mutual love and trust. His was in fact the rare kind of family in which both parents are capable of forgiveness.

Jesus needed this, for he was human as well as divine. If he was to grow into the man he was meant to become, he needed what people need, and do not always get: love and support and understanding, deep respect and trust and responsiveness.

It must have been wonderful beyond words for him to have, as he did in Joseph, a human father who was a model of love and trust and peace, as it was wonderful for him to have, as he did in Mary, a human mother who was the embodiment of love and grace and truth.

With them as his parents he could become the Jesus we know. That is something of what it meant for Jesus.

What does this story mean for us? Perhaps this is part of it: when we see Joseph being so amazingly trusted by God, we might find ourselves asking, "What about us? Are we trusted too?"

The answer is surely yes. I think God trusts each one of us, depends on each of us, for the fulfillment of his promise for the world. As St. Teresa said, Christ has no hands but ours.

Our God is not an autocratic figure giving orders and demanding obedience. He is the God who calls us constantly to open our hearts to his love, to his strength, and to his peace. He calls us to fulfill our humanity as his children, and he places everything in our hands. He trusts us, as he trusted Joseph. Our real question is: will we be worthy of that trust? Let us pray that we will.

When we hear the second part of the story, in which God sends an angel to help Joseph, we might ask, "How about us? Will God help us too? By sending us angels?"

I am sure he will help us, in a thousand ways, but whether by sending angels is a harder question, which each of us must answer on his or her own. For what it is worth, I myself think the world is full of angels, blessing us, guiding us, encouraging us—most of them in human form. We are sometimes even able to be angels for each other.

One last thing. To understand this story it is important to see that when the angel visits Joseph his aim is not to give him some new and unwelcome divine command, to make him do something unpleasant against his will. Quite the reverse: the idea is rather to free his will, by confirming and empowering his already existing love for the astonishing woman we know as Mary. In this he stands for all of us, who beneath all our sinfulness want nothing more than to live out of the center of love deep in our hearts.

Joseph's reward for answering the call of the angel is nothing less than the transformation of his whole existence in the blessed years in which he will live as Mary's husband and Jesus' human father. Joseph was blest beyond blessings, and perhaps we can be blest too, if like him we can tune ourselves to the deepest loves and truths within us, and live them out under the grace of God.

AMEN

Questions

1. The story of Joseph is indeed striking. When presented with Mary's wholly unexplained pregnancy he somehow knew something at the center of his being that enabled him not to expose Mary to humiliation and death, in accordance with the law, but to preserve her life. Can you imagine what kind of knowledge this was? Have you ever had knowledge of such a kind?

2. When Joseph takes Mary as his wife, making possible the wonderful family in which Jesus was raised, he knows something similar. Can you imagine what this was? Have you ever had knowledge of such a

kind? One thing that helped him was the visitation of the angel. Have you ever had an experience like that?

3. If you were to compose a prayer in response to this reading, what would it be?

11

Abraham and Nicodemus

We have three readings this week. The first is a passage from Genesis about Abraham's amazing willingness to respond to the call of Yahweh to leave his home forever and seek out the Promised Land. The second is a passage from Paul's letter to the Romans, about Abraham and the faith he exhibited. The third reading, from John, contains what may seem a mysterious colloquy between Jesus and Nicodemus, the Pharisee who has come to affirm his faith in him. As you read ask: how do these passages variously define faith? How do you define it?

In the passage from John, Nicodemus is what comics would call the "straight man," meaning the one who makes the expected remarks and responses; Jesus is the source of the apparent strangeness in what we read. As you read what Jesus says, ask yourself why he talks to Nicodemus as he does. What is he assuming about him? Is he right? How does he want Nicodemus to respond?

Where do you find yourself in these passages?

Genesis 12:1–8

Now the Lord said to Abram, "Go from your country and your kindred and your father's house to the land that I will show you. I will make of you a great nation, and I will bless you, and make your name great, so that you will be a blessing. I will bless those who bless you, and the one who curses you I will curse; and in you all the families of the earth shall be blessed."

So Abram went, as the Lord had told him; and Lot went with him. Abram was seventy-five years old when he departed from Haran. Abram took his wife Sarai and his brother's son Lot, and all the possessions that they had gathered, and the persons whom they had acquired in Haran; and they set forth to go to the land of Canaan.

When they had come to the land of Canaan, Abram passed through the land to the place at Shechem, to the oak of Moreh. At that time the Canaanites were in the land.

Then the Lord appeared to Abram, and said, "To your offspring I will give this land." So he built there an altar to the Lord, who had appeared to him. From there he moved on to the hill country on the east of Bethel, and pitched his tent, with Bethel on the west and Ai on the east; and there he built an altar to the Lord and invoked the name of the Lord.

The Letter to the Romans 4:1–5, 13–17

What then are we to say was gained by Abraham, our ancestor according to the flesh? For if Abraham was justified by works, he has something to boast about, but not before God. For what does the scripture say? "Abraham believed God, and it was reckoned to him as righteousness." Now to one who works, wages are not reckoned as a gift but as something due. But to one who without works trusts him who justifies the ungodly, such faith is reckoned as righteousness. For the promise that he would inherit the world did not come to Abraham or to his descendants through the law but through the righteousness of faith. If it is the adherents of the law who are to be the heirs, faith is null and the promise is void. For the law brings wrath; but where there is no law, neither is there violation. For this reason it depends on faith, in order that the promise may rest on grace and be guaranteed to all his descendants, not only to the adherents of the law but also to those who share the faith of Abraham (for he is the father of all of us, as it is written, "I have made you the father of many nations")—in the presence of the God in whom he believed, who gives life to the dead and calls into existence the things that do not exist.

The Gospel of John 3:1–11

Now there was a Pharisee named Nicodemus, a leader of the Jews. He came to Jesus by night and said to him, "Rabbi, we know that you are a teacher who has come from God; for no one can do these signs that you do apart from the presence of God."

Jesus answered him, "Very truly, I tell you, no one can see the kingdom of God without being born from above." Nicodemus said to him, "How can anyone be born after having grown old? Can one enter a second time into the mother's womb and be born?"

Jesus answered, "Very truly, I tell you, no one can enter the kingdom of God without being born of water and Spirit. What is born of the flesh is flesh, and what is born of the Spirit is spirit. Do not be astonished that I said to you, 'You must be born from above.' The wind blows where it chooses, and you hear the sound of it, but you do not know where it comes from or where it goes. So it is with everyone who is born of the Spirit."

Nicodemus said to him, "How can these things be?"

Jesus answered him, "Are you a teacher of Israel, and yet you do not understand these things? Very truly, I tell you, we speak of what we know and testify to what we have seen; yet you do not receive our testimony.

"If I have told you about earthly things and you do not believe, how can you believe if I tell you about heavenly things? No one has ascended into heaven except the one who descended from heaven, the Son of Man. And just as Moses lifted up the serpent in the wilderness, so must the Son of Man be lifted up, that whoever believes in him may have eternal life.

"For God so loved the world that he gave his only Son, that everyone who believes in him may not perish but have eternal life."

The Church of the Mediator, March 20, 2011

May the words of my mouth and the meditations of my heart be always acceptable in thy sight, O Lord, my strength and my redeemer.

The readings we heard today are all about faith, a topic that raises familiar and difficult questions. What is faith? Where does it come from? When do we have enough, or the right kind? What happens if we don't have enough, or the right kind? How is faith related to the gift of eternal life?

Let's start with Abraham, who is presented as a model of faith. At this stage in his story we know essentially nothing about him. As far as we know he is just a man called Abram—a name that will be later changed to Abraham—living in what is now southern Iraq. With no warning at all, out of the blue, God speaks to him, saying in essence, "Leave your country, leave your father's house, leave your family, and go to a place that I will show you. If you do, I will make you a great nation."

We do not know why God chose Abram; we do not even know how God spoke to him—face to face?—or how Abram knew it was God speaking, or how it was that Abram could bring himself to obey this voice, but he did. Although Abram was seventy-five years old, he picked up and took his family he knew not where. Talk about an act of faith! Who would do such a thing?

In his letter to the Romans, Paul is talking about a different moment in Abraham's life: when God promises him that he will have a son, even though he is over ninety, and that his descendants will be as numerous as the stars in the sky. The writer of Genesis says that Abraham "believed the Lord; and the Lord reckoned it to him as righteousness." Paul says that it was Abraham's faith that justified him; and likewise that it is our faith—not the law, not our works—that justifies all of us. (As you know, this teaching will be the foundation of Protestantism fifteen hundred years later.)

Of course the gospel is about faith too, the faith of Nicodemus. Think what happens to him: he comes to Jesus, at night, secretly, to say that he knows that Jesus comes from God. He knows this because the miracles prove it. This is an act of faith, and from Nicodemus' point of view it is a brave and radical act, for he is going directly against the powerful community of the Pharisees to which he belongs. That is why he comes secretly, at night.

But instead of welcoming Nicodemus, Jesus tells him a series of mysterious things. You must be born from above, born of water and the Spirit. The Spirit blows where it chooses, and you hear the sound of it, but you do not know where it comes from or where it goes. This is how it is with those born of the Spirit. *"If I have told you about earthly things and you do not believe, how can you believe if I tell you about heavenly things?"*

The gospel passage is a puzzling story. Nicodemus *does* believe in Jesus, and comes to tell him so, but Jesus says that that kind of belief is not enough.

It is not enough for you to say that you know I "come from God," Jesus tells him; something else must happen, something that language cannot capture: you must be born from above, or born again; you must be born of the spirit and the water; you must live in the world where the spirit blows where it chooses, where you will know where it comes from and where it is going.

Jesus is saying that the faith required of Nicodemus, and of each of us, is not just the affirmation of a belief but the transformation of the self. Nicodemus is not yet there, and we may not be there either.

In fact, Nicodemus will get there, as he shows later in the Gospel of John when he stands up publicly for Jesus against the Pharisees, saying that he is entitled to a fair trial, and still later when he brings one hundred pounds of ointment to the tomb to anoint Jesus' body. In doing these things Nicodemus shows that he does not just "believe" in Jesus; he has given himself to him, in love and courage. He has been born from above.

How about us? We are being told that "belief" or "faith" is not a simple matter of yes or no, not a matter of decision or choice, not a simple affirmation, but a process with many stages, ever deepening, ever transforming. None of us is at the end of the process; none of us has perfect faith; every one of us has far to go. Faith and belief are not decisions; they are transformations, and they are never completed. Like Nicodemus we need to be born from above. How can this happen?

At the end of the passage Jesus sums up a whole theology of belief, saying, "*God so loved the world that he gave his only Son, that everyone who believes in him may not perish but may have eternal life.*"

This is comforting language, for it affirms that God loves the world, loves his creation, and loves us. That is good. But in another way it is not comforting at all, for it implies that eternal life is given only to those who "believe in him." What does this mean? What kind of belief counts?

Jesus has made clear that Nicodemus does not qualify, or not yet. Certainly it is not enough for us just to go to church on Sunday and recite the Creed. Something much deeper is required. So what is faith? What is belief? Where does it come from? How do we know if we have enough, or the right kind?

As a starting point, it may help us think about this to know that the Greek word that is translated as *faith* or *belief* actually has a root meaning different from either of those words: its root meaning is *trust*, a word with quite different overtones and implications.

Think of what happens, for example, when someone asks us, or we ask ourselves, in the familiar way, "Why do you believe in God?" This question often begins a process of thought that is not fruitful. We find ourselves making arguments that we hope will explain why we think God exists—arguments, say, based on the design of the creation; or the need for a first mover, to explain the act of creation itself; or the infallibility of Scripture; or something else we can find in standard theological treatises. But none of these arguments is going to persuade anybody who does not already believe, and, for most of us, they do not begin to express the nature of our own experience and commitment. This line of thought is a detour into an empty place.

The word *trust* works very differently. It does not invoke an intellectual operation, but a giving of the self. It is not a calculation of probability, but the affirmation of what is deepest within us, the ground on which we stand in an uncertain world. It is not a statement of a proposition, but a social action: "I put my trust in you."

Suppose that when we recited the Nicene Creed (as we soon will) we used a more literal translation of the Greek in which it was written and said not "We believe" but "We trust": "We trust in one God, the Father, the Almighty, maker of heaven and earth. . . . We trust in one Lord, Jesus

Christ, the only Son of God. . . . We trust in the Holy Spirit, the Lord, the giver of life."

Do you see how different that would be? A lot of philosophical and theological distress would simply disappear. To think of faith in terms of trust, rather than belief, would lead to thought and conversation not about the probability of God's existence, but about the nature and depth of our soul's commitment.

To think of faith in terms of trust might also help us understand Abraham. He does not have an abstract belief, a set of philosophical positions, but something very different: real trust in God.

Trust is what Paul has, too, when he sets forth on his incredible, impossible, successful ministry. Trust is what Nicodemus does *not* have at the beginning, when he is merely affirming a belief—when he says, as a kind of empirical scientist, "I know you come from God because of the miracles you do"—and trust is what he *does* have when he stands up to the Pharisees and when he brings the ointment to the tomb. Trust is a ground of action in a soul transformed.

In all the people we heard about today, trust in God is the basis of a new life. It expresses itself in speech and action, in new relations with others, in a new sense of one's own soul and of the possibilities of life. It may even be that the life of faith, defined as trust in God, is itself the eternal life of which Jesus speaks.

Where does trust of this kind come from? It cannot be manufactured by us; it is not the result of an act of will or choice; it is a gift, a gift of grace, offered I believe to all the world. Our task is to prepare ourselves for it by thought and prayer, to perceive it when it first emerges, to accept it joyfully and confidently, and to try to learn to live out of it, to live in the discipline it offers us.

Will we succeed? Certainly not, or not perfectly. But life is change and growth, and as Paul told us a few Sundays ago, "[N]either the one who plants nor the one who waters is anything, but only God, who gives the growth" (1 Cor 3:7). So we may have hope. All growth comes from God.

With Abraham we should listen for the call from above, for the call from within. With Paul we should hope to reach out to others. And with Nicodemus we should hope to learn how a faith that begins in tentative mental affirmation, a kind of struggle of belief, can end in a trust that transforms the soul—a trust that leads us into new life.

AMEN

Questions

1. First a clarification. When Paul distinguishes between the law and faith, saying that Abraham was moved by faith, not the law, one thing he has in mind is that at the time of Abraham there was in fact no law: no Torah, no ten commandments, no Sabbath, not even the ritual of circumcision until Abraham was commanded to circumcise his sons (Genesis 10:17). For Paul, Abraham is a model of faith who comes before there is any law; he is thus, perhaps surprisingly, a model for us who come after the law, that is, in the world Jesus has entered and transformed. For us, as for Abraham, what matters is not compliance with the law but faith. (Paul's not so hidden concern is to resist those who believe that a person can become a Christian only if he or she accepts the law of Moses, including the requirement, for men, of circumcision.)

2. Think now of your own experience of faith. What is faith, as you know it? How does it move you? These are puzzling questions for many of us. Does it help to ask whether there is there any analogy in your life to the faith of Abraham, which led him to travel to a foreign country far away, or to the faith of Paul, who went through the whole of the eastern Mediterranean to establish churches, or to the faith of Nicodemus, who stood up to the Pharisees on Jesus' behalf and brought ointment to the tomb?

    What is faith?

3. Where in your experience, or as you imagine it, does faith come from? Is it a decision, a revelation, an inner judgment, a gift of grace, or what? (All of the above?) Is there some way you can give yourself faith?

4. Now think about the relation between these three passages. They are very different from one another in context, audience, purpose, voice, feeling, and style, as well as in the kind of truth to which they make a claim. How can such different things belong in the same sacred book? Is this kind of difference a source of undesirable incoherence in our sacred text or is it a gift and blessing?

12

"I Am in My Father, and You in Me, and I in You"

Once more we have multiple readings, this time Paul's speech to the Athenians (from the Acts of the Apostles) and one of Jesus' speeches to his friends in the Gospel of John. These are in some ways very different passages, with different authors, audiences, and occasions. As you read them do you see any points of similarity or analogy between them? In particular you might ask how each passage defines God, asking yourself each time whether this how you think of him. How *do* you think of him—or her?

Acts of the Apostles 17:22-31

Then Paul stood in front of the Areopagus and said, "Athenians, I see how extremely religious you are in every way. For as I went through the city and looked carefully at the objects of your worship, I found among them an altar with the inscription, 'To an unknown god.' What therefore you worship as unknown, this I proclaim to you.

"The God who made the world and everything in it, he who is Lord of heaven and earth, does not live in shrines made by human hands, nor is he served by human hands, as though he needed anything, since he himself gives to all mortals life and breath and all things. From one ancestor he made all nations to inhabit the whole earth, and he allotted the times of their existence and the boundaries of the places where they would live, so that they would search for God and perhaps grope for him and find him—though indeed he is not far from each one of us.

"For 'In him we live and move and have our being'; as even some of your own poets have said, 'For we too are his offspring.' Since we are God's offspring, we ought not to think that the deity is like gold, or silver, or stone, an image formed by the art and imagination of mortals. While God has overlooked the times of human ignorance, now he commands all people everywhere to repent, because he has fixed a day on which he will have the world judged in righteousness by a man whom he has appointed, and of this he has given assurance to all by raising him from the dead."

The Gospel of John 14:15–21

"If you love me, you will keep my commandments. And I will ask the Father, and he will give you another Advocate, to be with you forever. This is the Spirit of truth, whom the world cannot receive, because it neither sees him nor knows him. You know him, because he abides with you, and he will be in you.

"I will not leave you orphaned; I am coming to you. In a little while the world will no longer see me, but you will see me; because I live, you also will live. On that day you will know that I am in my Father, and you in me, and I in you.

"They who have my commandments and keep them are those who love me; and those who love me will be loved by my Father, and I will love them and reveal myself to them."

The Church of the Mediator, May 29, 2011

May the words of my mouth and the meditations of my heart be always acceptable in thy sight, O Lord, my strength and my redeemer.

IN OUR READINGS TODAY we heard Jesus speaking to his friends, just before his death, and Paul speaking to the Athenians. They both raise the same immense question: how do we, how can we, how ought we to imagine God? The answer, in both cases, is surprising and powerful.

Let us start with Paul's speech about the God, the Christian God, whom he has come to proclaim to the Athenians. Obviously Paul had a hard job, and there is much to say about the way he does it. But today I want to focus on a single famous moment, towards the end, when (apparently quoting a Greek poet) he says this about God: "in him we live and move and have our being."

In a similar way I want to focus on two very small parts of Jesus' speech to his disciples. First, in speaking about the Advocate whom the Father will send to them after Jesus departs—the Spirit of Truth—Jesus says that the disciples will see and recognize the Spirit, as the world will not, "*because he abides with you, and he will be in you.*" Later Jesus says that when he comes again "*You will know that I am in my Father, and you in me, and I in you.*"

In these brief phrases Jesus and Paul are both imagining God in an extraordinary way. They are telling us that God is in us, and that we are in God. This is a shocking way to think of God: shocking to the Greeks, to the Jews, and I think to us too. For Jesus and Paul are not speaking in the traditional way, as if God and the human person were two completely separate beings, as the Old Testament speaks about Yahweh, the God of Sinai, for example, or as the Greeks speak about Zeus, who dwells on Olympus. Rather both are imagining God and human beings as somehow existing inside each other: the Spirit "*abides with you and will be in you,*" says Jesus; when I come again "*you will know that I am in my Father, and you in me, and I in you.*" "In him," says Paul, "we live and move and have our being."

Both of these people are imagining God as infinitely close, constantly surrounding us, alive deep within us. This is in a sense familiar, but it is not, I think, how we usually imagine God. As Christians we believe that Jesus was God in the flesh among us, but he has risen and ascended. In the Lord's Prayer, God is in heaven. According to our usual beliefs, the Holy Spirit is indeed with us, but we do not talk about the Spirit very much.

There is an important element of distance built into our usual way of religious thinking, distance across which we try to reach and across which we imagine God reaching. Much of what we do is meant to bring us closer to God, or God closer to us. We do not have temples in which the Deity dwells, as the Greeks and the Jews did, but we do have special buildings called churches, like this beautiful church, in which we feel that God is especially present; we do not have animal sacrifices as ways of connecting to God, as both Greeks and Jews did, but we do celebrate the wonderful sacrifice that ended sacrifices, that of Christ on the Cross; we do not have the Law of Sinai, through which God reached out to his people, but we do have a different and to us much better law, the law of love; we do not have the religious regulations of Leviticus, but we do have the commandments of the Gospel and, as Episcopalians, we have the forms of the Book of Common Prayer, which do much to give shape to our devotional life. In our Eucharist, which we celebrate today, we praise God, we give thanks to God, we bring God our petitions, we confess our sinfulness to him, we accept the living presence of Christ in the sacrament, and we say or sing Hallelujah.

All of these are ways of reaching across the distance between us and God, ways that we often feel bring us closer to him. In engaging in them we inhabit a deep and complex and rich religious culture, and thank God for it. They are wonderful things, immense gifts to us.

But this is not what Jesus and Paul are talking about. When we say that our religious practices and culture "bring us closer to God" we are implying that we start away from God. He is apart from us, and we approach him from a distance.

Jesus and Paul are saying that we have already reached him, and that he has already reached us. This is an incredibly, unimaginably intimate vision of God. God is not remote and distant from us, on a mountain or in the sky, but within us, actually inside each of us; and we are within him, within the God in whom we live and move and have our being.

This is not just loose or metaphorical talk. We are being told that God is inside us, all the time, every day, however we feel, whatever we do, and that we live surrounded by him, held by him, all the time, every day, however we feel, whatever we do. And in all this he loves us.

I have heard the language Paul used a thousand times I suppose, but without ever thinking much about it. This time, as I did think about it, I was stunned.

Suppose we really did know, all the time, that God was in us, that we were in God: what would that mean?

I think it would mean the end of all our anxiety and fear, the end of all our false goals and idols, the end of our empty aims and desires, which are our substitutes for God. It would mean open and easy service to others, the ready giving up of what we have and who we are. The Voice within us would speak, and we would gladly respond. How could we not?

This transformation would happen not only in church but in our darkest hours, in the night watches, in frantic crowds, in the morass of what would otherwise be despair. Our lives would be full to the brim of hope and joy. What else could we possibly want? This is a wonderful prospect.

But here is the problem, at least for me: do I in fact recognize that God is in me and I am in God? That it is God in whom I live and move and have my being? The answer for me, most of the time, is no, and that may be true for you as well. I need the rituals and stories and buildings and communities that I feel bring me somewhat closer to God, the apparatus that enables me to be at once close to him and distant from him.

These two passages thus put into tension two ways of thinking about, imagining, and responding to God: first, as the Athenians do, as the Jews do, and as we Episcopalians do most of the time, namely, as a God we are often distant from, or who is distant from us, a God we can sometimes approach, who sometimes approaches us; and, second, as those other people do who really know, in their hearts, all the time, that God is within them, that they are within God. So what do we do with this tension?

What I called our rich religious culture, with its texts and songs and stories, its rituals and buildings, its forms and constraints, is wonderful. All of it can be expressive of God, bring us closer to God, no question about it. But these things can also become, against our intentions, a denial of the presence of the living God within us, around us, all the time, here and now, in this room, in our hearts. They can in fact be substitutes for the God who lives within us, within whom we live. They can blind us to that reality. They can be ways in which we think we are moving closer to God but actually maintaining our distance from him. That may even be part of our purpose.

Yet if we were to try to live simply out of the knowledge of God within us, around us, that would not work. Our knowledge would fade or become distorted. We would lose our bearings.

It seems that we need both, both the rituals that bring us closer to God, as it were from a distance, and the knowledge that he is already within us. We need the rituals because they call us back to God. Without them we might even lose the sense of God within us, God around us, God in our neighbor. But we also need to have the living sense that God is in us, that we are in God, and bring that sense to our ritual life, or that life may be stale and dead.

How can we attune ourselves to this double truth, this double reality? In particular, how can we live out of the truth that God is in us, that we are in God?

I don't have any ready answer, but one place to begin might be right here, and right now, with our experience of the church, this church and the larger church, not so much as rite and ritual but as community. If the church is healthy, as this one is, we can often feel and see that we are in the presence of a love greater than human love, outside us and within us—in the people next to us at the service, in the people serving coffee, in the people caring for the grounds and maintaining the altar in all its beauty, in the people facing the practical questions the church must address about money and buildings, in the people teaching children in the church school, and in the people who in Milton's great phrase only stand and wait—and also in our own response to these people and what they do.

Of course it is not only in church that this can happen: we can see God in the kindness of the bus driver who helps a disabled person onto the bus, in the courage of a teenager who stands up for a friend against the crowd, in the absorbing love of a mother for a child, in the alert attention a teacher gives to the people in his or her charge. It is not only in Christians that God can be found, and not only Christians who live in him.

If we look at our own daily and ordinary experiences with open eyes and hearts, then, we may find, to our surprise, that God is in fact present and at work in what we have always considered unremarkable parts of life, the ordinary stuff of existence: in us, around us, and in other people too. We may suddenly see something right before us that we never really noticed, and know that this is God.

In such a way we may hope, sometimes at least, to have direct and personal experience of the God that is in us; of the God that is in others; of the God in whom we live and move and have our being.

AMEN

Questions

1. Both Paul and John are talking about the inwardness of God, the fact that God in some way is within us. Does this possibility correspond with your own experience? That is, do you ever have the sense that God is within you? If so, can you simply build your life on that sense, or do you need something else as well?

2. They are also saying that we are in God: "in him we live and move and have our being." Does this possibility correspond with your own experience? That is, do you ever have the sense that you are in God, surrounded by God? If so, can you simply build your life on that sense, or do you need something else as well?

3. Think about the rites and rituals of the Church, the sacraments, the traditions, the music. Do these bring you closer to God? What would you do without them? Do you need anything else?

4. If you were to compose a prayer after reading these two passages, what would it be?

13

"I Am with You Always, to the End of the Age"

Again we have several readings, this time the creation story from Genesis and two farewells: Paul's farewell to the people of Corinth, and the resurrected Jesus' farewell to his disciples. As you read them, try to imagine what these last two readings can possibly have to do with the beautiful story of creation in Genesis. Remember also to make note of the questions that emerge for you as you work through this material.

Genesis 1:1–24a

In the beginning when God created the heavens and the earth, the earth was a formless void and darkness covered the face of the deep, while a wind from God swept over the face of the waters.

Then God said, "Let there be light"; and there was light. And God saw that the light was good; and God separated the light from the darkness. God called the light Day, and the darkness he called Night. And there was evening and there was morning, the first day.

And God said, "Let there be a dome in the midst of the waters, and let it separate the waters from the waters." So God made the dome and separated the waters that were under the dome from the waters that were above the dome. And it was so. God called the dome Sky. And there was evening and there was morning, the second day.

And God said, "Let the waters under the sky be gathered together into one place, and let the dry land appear." And it was so. God called the dry land Earth, and the waters that were gathered together he called Seas. And God saw that it was good.

Then God said, "Let the earth put forth vegetation: plants yielding seed, and fruit trees of every kind on earth that bear fruit with the seed in it." And it was so. The earth brought forth vegetation: plants yielding seed of every kind, and trees of every kind bearing fruit with the seed in it. And God saw that it was good. And there was evening and there was morning, the third day.

And God said, "Let there be lights in the dome of the sky to separate the day from the night; and let them be for signs and for seasons and for days and years, and let them be lights in the dome of the sky to give light upon the earth." And it was so. God made the two great lights—the greater light to rule the day and the lesser light to rule the night—and the stars. God set them in the dome of the sky to give light upon the earth, to rule over the day and over the night, and to separate the light from the darkness. And God saw that it was good. And there was evening and there was morning, the fourth day.

And God said, "Let the waters bring forth swarms of living creatures, and let birds fly above the earth across the dome of the sky." So God created the great sea monsters and every living creature that moves, of every kind, with which the waters swarm, and every winged bird of every kind. And God saw that it was good. God blessed them, saying, "Be fruitful and multiply and fill the waters in the seas, and let birds multiply on the earth." And there was evening and there was morning, the fifth day.

And God said, "Let the earth bring forth living creatures of every kind: cattle and creeping things and wild animals of the earth of every kind." And it was so. God made the wild animals of the earth of every kind, and the cattle of every kind, and everything that creeps upon the ground of every kind. And God saw that it was good.

Then God said, "Let us make humankind in our image, according to our likeness; and let them have dominion over the fish of the sea, and over the birds of the air, and over the cattle, and over all the wild animals of the earth, and over every creeping thing that creeps upon the earth." So God created humankind in his image, in the image of God he created them; male and female he created them. God blessed them, and God said to them, "Be fruitful and multiply, and fill the earth and subdue it; and have dominion over the fish of the sea and over the birds of the air and over every living thing that moves upon the earth."

God said, "See, I have given you every plant yielding seed that is upon the face of all the earth, and every tree with seed in its fruit; you shall have them for food. And to every beast of the earth, and to every bird of the air, and to everything that creeps on the earth, everything that has the breath of life, I have given every green plant for food." And it was so.

God saw everything that he had made, and indeed, it was very good. And there was evening and there was morning, the sixth day.

Thus the heavens and the earth were finished, and all their multitude. And on the seventh day God finished the work that he had done, and he rested on the seventh day from all the work that he had done. So God blessed the seventh day and hallowed it, because on it God rested from all the work that he had done in creation.

These are the generations of the heavens and the earth when they were created.

Second Corinthians 13:11–13

Finally, brothers and sisters, farewell. Put things in order, listen to my appeal, agree with one another, live in peace; and the God of love and peace will be with you. Greet one another with a holy kiss. All the saints greet you. The grace of the Lord Jesus Christ, the love of God, and the communion of the Holy Spirit be with all of you.

The Gospel of Matthew 28:16–20

> Now the eleven disciples went to Galilee, to the mountain to which Jesus had directed them. When they saw him, they worshiped him; but some doubted. And Jesus came and said to them, "All authority in heaven and on earth has been given to me. Go therefore and make disciples of all nations, baptizing them in the name of the Father and of the Son and of the Holy Spirit, and teaching them to obey everything that I have commanded you. And remember, I am with you always, to the end of the age."

The Church of the Mediator, June 19, 2011

May the words of my mouth and the meditations of my heart be always acceptable in thy sight, O Lord, my strength and my redeemer.

The passage from Genesis we just heard is one of the most beautiful things in the Bible: the story of the creation of a wonderful universe by a loving God.

This story is full of the sense that everything in the created world is good, or very good, as God says at end when he contemplates his handiwork as a whole. There is no evil in this world. No one kills anything. Even the animals do not eat each other, but like the human beings live on grasses and fruits. There is no sin. God blesses the man and the woman, and bids them multiply. All is good.

We sometimes have a similar experience of essential goodness and wholeness in our own lives, often at certain moments of beginning. Think what we feel at the beginning of a healthy human life, for example, when a baby is born to loving parents. All is good. There is no evil. The baby and his parents are very good, as God might say.

The Bible will not continue in this vein. What comes next is a second telling of the creation story, this time with Adam and Eve's disobedience to God, their expulsion from Paradise to lives of pain and labor. Then we are told of sinful humanity, of the Flood, of slavery in Egypt, of the Exodus across the desert, of the worship of the golden calf, of apparently endless wars, of the Babylonian captivity, and finally of the return to Jerusalem.

We may begin in perfection, but we live our lives out in imperfection. This is what the Old Testament tells us.

This pattern occurs in our own lives too, of course. The perfect child will grow up in an imperfect world, will confront sorrow and loss and failure, will confront his or her own sinfulness, as we all have had to do. Human maturity is not perfection, even when its beginnings seem perfect.

The New Testament teaches us a similar lesson. It begins with the wonderful story of Jesus' birth. Everything is bright and shining at this glorious moment of perfection, and rightly so. We feel it every Christmas. But the story yet to come will include things that are very hard, sometimes horrible. Jesus himself will face hostility, contempt, abuse, and finally death on the Cross. At the very lowest moment, after Jesus has been killed, he rises from the dead, and everything looks wonderful again. We begin anew. We have the unalloyed joy of Easter matching the unalloyed joy of Christmas, and we feel it strongly, as we ought to do.

But this new and joyful beginning is in turn followed by the reality of imperfection. When Jesus departs once more, the disciples, and we, must learn that the world is still full of sin, that we are still full of sin, and that all the evils and difficulties of life still have to be faced.

In both parts of the Bible, then, and also in the structure of each human life, we see a deep rhythm: from a new beginning in perfect joy to the realities of danger and difficulty and evil—and maybe, just maybe, then to a kind of mature acceptance of ourselves and the conditions of our lives.

Indeed this rhythm is repeated in the shape of the single day, moving from the fresh beginning of dawn, through maturing complications, to what we hope is the relative serenity and reconciliation of evening.

It is at an evening of their lives that both Paul and Jesus speak to us in today's readings, as they say farewell to their friends.

Paul is speaking to the church in Corinth: the church with which he had struggled so mightily for so long, the church that had been so difficult and ill-behaved and frustrating. Corinth was for Paul a piece of real life, where things did not work out as well as he wanted. The Corinthians were difficult people.

Paul shows us how to say farewell to such a community, at the end of such a life: not with bitterness but with enduring love and acceptance. He has moved from a beginning full of freshness and hope, through disappointments and failures and woundedness, into something far deeper, a kind of mature and accepting love of others and himself.

This is what he says: "Finally, brothers and sisters, farewell. Put things in order, listen to my appeal, agree with one another, live in peace; and the God of love and peace will be with you. Greet one another with a holy kiss. All the saints greet you. The grace of the Lord Jesus Christ, the love of God, and the communion of the Holy Spirit be with all of you."

This is a model of mature and sustained love.

Jesus, too, is saying goodbye. The words we heard today are in fact the last words of the Gospel of Matthew, Jesus' closing words to his disciples.

The disciples are in a moment of crisis, facing the end of one thing, the presence of Jesus on earth, and the beginning of something else, life without him in the world as it is, full of danger and evil. This is a beginning, and it is full of possibility and hope, but also of doubt and fear. We are told in fact that some of the disciples doubted.

What Jesus says to his friends is more difficult to hear than what Paul says, for he makes demands of his friends that must have seemed impossible: "*All authority in heaven and on earth has been given to me. Go therefore and make disciples of all nations, baptizing them in the name of the Father and of the Son and of the Holy Spirit, and teaching them to obey everything that I have commanded you.*"

This is very impressive, especially in the confidence Jesus shows in his friends. But think of this from the point of view of the disciples, who are about to be deprived of Jesus' presence on earth, the most important thing in life. How is this tiny group of ordinary people from Palestine to go through the whole world baptizing and proclaiming the death and resurrection of Jesus? How can they possibly do that? It must have seemed utterly impossible.

Equally difficult, in a different way, is Jesus' injunction: "*Teach them to obey everything I have commanded you.*" The problem here is that the Jesus we know does not characteristically issue commandments and demand obedience. He just doesn't. That is what the God of the Old Testament does. That God gives the commandments at Sinai, he creates a whole body of law that his people are to follow, he expects obedience, and he punishes the people when they fail.

But Jesus is not like that. In fact, in Matthew especially, Jesus spends a lot of time energetically resisting the "command and obey" image of God that the Pharisees have, an image that results in the legalism that Jesus rejects.

Think of what Jesus has actually said and done in Matthew's Gospel, for example. I won't try to summarize the whole thing, but here are some characteristic events. Jesus has announced the presence of the kingdom of heaven. He has cured the sick. He has told us, blessed are the poor, the meek, the pure of heart, the peacemakers. He has told us that anger is a sin, just like murder, that lust is a sin, just like adultery. He has said, if someone strikes your right cheek, turn him the other also. Love your enemies and pray for those who persecute you. He has given us a string of parables to express what the kingdom of heaven is like: like a sower whose seeds fall on different kinds of ground, like a field with wheat and tares, like a mustard seed, like a pearl beyond price.

Little of this takes the form of commandments, and what does take that form is impossible for us to obey. Who can be without anger, or love his enemies?

The commandment that Jesus emphasizes the most is the great commandment: to love God with our whole hearts and minds and souls and to love our neighbors as ourselves. We know we cannot actually do those things. We can try, but we will fail. As we confess every Sunday, "We have not loved you with our whole heart, and we have not loved our neighbors as ourselves." We never will. In fact, Jesus asks us over and over to do what we know we cannot do, to be what we cannot be. That is a central characteristic of his ministry.

So how can the disciples go out to tell the nations to obey the commandments of Jesus? Why does Jesus tell them to do that?

I am not sure, but I think that in this speech Jesus is trying to equip his disciples, and us, for life in the world as it will be after he is gone, with all its difficulties and evils. When he talks of "obeying his commandments," I do not think he has suddenly become the kind of Pharisee he resisted so strenuously, but in a shorthand way is saying something like this: "As you make your way in the world after I am gone, trying to create the church, you should take to heart everything I have said and done, from healing to parables to the great commandments to love God and your neighbor."

The moment at which Jesus speaks to the disciples is a great beginning, for the disciples and for us, but not an easy one. We know hard things are on the way. It is as a way of dealing with this fact that Jesus is telling all of us to remember faithfully all that he has said and done, puzzling and challenging as so much of it is. That is what we can count on to help us through what is coming.

At the end Jesus adds one thing, a crucial thing, telling us that as we struggle to live out his gift, his love, in a world full of difficulty and evil, we are not alone. We not only have the memory of what he has said and done, but we have him—here, now, with us, within us. His love, like Paul's, reaches out to us over the centuries, offering us a new ground of life: "*I am with you always, to the end of the age.*"

AMEN

Questions

1. Can you locate, in your own life, experiences that have the sequence described above, moving from a joyful beginning into an imperfect life, full of frustration and sin, and then to a place of relative peace and acceptance? How did you get to that final place?

2. One point of the first creation story in Genesis is to provide a mythic explanation of the institution of the Sabbath, the first of God's works that he calls holy. In a way that is the climax: God created, then rested, so we in our ways are to create, and then rest. As a church or temple is a physical space devoted to God, and in this way made holy, the Sabbath is a period of time that is similarly sanctified.

Do you have experience of this kind of Sabbath? What does the Sabbath do? Can you explain how and why it is important? Here you might want to look at a lovely book by Abraham Heschel, *The Sabbath* (1951), which is an explanation of what the Sabbath means in Jewish life and belief. What does the Sabbath mean, what should it mean, in Christian life and belief?

3. Think now of your own experience of saying hello and goodbye: to other people, to moments in your life, to whole phases or stages in your life, to institutions or roles. How do you say goodbye? Do Paul and Jesus have something to teach us here?

14

Jesus' Imagistic Thinking

This time we have Jesus the teacher, telling parables. Our questions are: what is a parable, and why does Jesus choose to speak that way? Why does he not just say whatever is on his mind directly and plainly, instead of resorting to these images? By speaking in parables what is he telling us about the way we should think and talk about the kingdom of God?

You might ask yourself this as well: do you ever speak in parables, or similar forms? When, and why?

The Gospel of Matthew 13:31–33, 44–50

He put before them another parable: "The kingdom of heaven is like a mustard seed that someone took and sowed in his field; it is the smallest of all the seeds, but when it has grown it is the greatest of shrubs and becomes a tree, so that the birds of the air come and make nests in its branches."

He told them another parable: "The kingdom of heaven is like yeast that a woman took and mixed in with three measures of flour until all of it was leavened."

"The kingdom of heaven is like treasure hidden in a field, which someone found and hid; then in his joy he goes and sells all that he has and buys that field.

"Again, the kingdom of heaven is like a merchant in search of fine pearls; on finding one pearl of great value, he went and sold all that he had and bought it.

"Again, the kingdom of heaven is like a net that was thrown into the sea and caught fish of every kind; when it was full, they drew it ashore, sat down, and put the good into baskets but threw out the bad.

"So it will be at the end of the age. The angels will come out and separate the evil from the righteous and throw them into the furnace of fire, where there will be weeping and gnashing of teeth."

The Church of the Mediator, July 24, 2011

May the words of my mouth and the meditations of my heart be always acceptable in thy sight, O Lord, my strength and my redeemer.

In today's Gospel, Jesus tells his followers a series of parables, all meant to explain the kingdom of heaven. It is like a mustard seed, he says, like yeast, like treasure hidden in a field, like a merchant in search of fine pearls, like a fishing net that brings in lots of different kinds of fish.

Why does Jesus talk in this oblique and imagistic way? Why does he not just describe the kingdom of heaven, and tell us what it is?

One answer is obvious: our language does not permit us simply to define and describe God, or his kingdom, as we might describe a car engine, say, or an elm tree. God is beyond our grasp, in some sense beyond our imagining, and certainly beyond our language. If we could pigeonhole him with definitions and descriptions, we would be exercising a kind of control over him, and that we can never do.

So Jesus speaks another way, in images and little stories. He does not tell us what the kingdom of heaven *is*, because that is impossible; instead he tells us what it is *like*, using a series of images to do so.

These images do not have single clear meanings, but multiple and often cryptic meanings. Take the mustard seed, for example. It is clear that in this little story something large and beautiful grows out of something infinitesimally small, by a process that is natural but also mysterious. But what does that seed represent? Is it the Word? Is it Jesus? Is it the faith of an individual person? The faith of the church? All of the above? We are given no answer.

Or think of the story of the woman kneading yeast into flour to make bread. Is it significant that the growth here is not simply a natural process, as with the mustard seed, but the achievement of skilled human action? Why? Is it significant that what is produced is food? That it is a woman, not a man, who is at work here? And what is the yeast anyway: the Word or faith or the church?

The parables about the treasure and the pearl are odd, for both stories seem to validate the impulse of human greed, of which we do not normally approve. In the treasure story, the actor finds the treasure, hides it on someone else's land, then buys the land, exulting in his cleverness. In the pearl story the merchant sells everything else to buy this one object. What is going on? How is this like the kingdom? It is never explained.

In the story about the fish in the net, Jesus does give us an interpretation, but to me it is rather odd and not very satisfactory. He says that as the fishermen throw away the useless fish and keep the valuable fish, so the angels will come on the last day and separate the evil from the righteous and throw them into the fire.

If we did not have that interpretation I don't think we would read it that way. Maybe we would begin by saying that the diversity of fish in the net is like the diversity of human life, which is immense and a very good thing. Maybe we would say that the fishermen choose only what they need for food and livelihood, and they choose well, mercifully and wisely. The rest of the fish they do not destroy, but set free. This is what the kingdom of God is like, one might say, full of diversity, good sense, and compassion.

So what on earth do we do with Jesus' interpretation? We will come back to this problem.

Notice that Jesus does not give us just one parable. He gives us a whole string of parables, one after the other, all of which are more or less obscure. We are dizzied by the sequence, thrown off balance, at once stimulated and confused. We have a natural impulse to turn the images into lessons of some kind, but this impulse is frustrated by the multiplicity and richness of significance of the stories. We cannot reliably translate them into propositions.

That is part of their point. The parables cannot bear that kind of weight. They have another kind of meaning. No translation can explain them. They are not about propositional truth but another kind of truth.

They open up like Japanese paper flowers placed in water.

I think that in telling us these parables Jesus is teaching us a way of being and acting in the world.

What is this way of being and acting? It is the life of the parable maker. The parables are performances of imagistic reasoning, and I think Jesus wants us to use this mode of thought too, not just as readers but as thinkers and speakers. If we are to bring the full powers of our minds and imaginations into the service of God we are to become parable makers ourselves, in imitation of him.

You may sensibly ask, "Parables? Parable making? How can you and I make parables?" Maybe it is not quite as impossible as we think. Let's try.

> —*The kingdom of heaven is like a swim in Lake Michigan on a summer afternoon.*
>
> —*The kingdom of heaven is like a father and his teenage son walking down a country road in October.*
>
> —*The kingdom of heaven is like a stranger stopping to help someone with a flat tire, perhaps someone of a different race or ethnicity.*
>
> —*The kingdom of heaven is like a bus driver welcoming passengers on a sleety February morning.*
>
> —*The kingdom of heaven is like picking basil or parsley for tonight's supper.*

Do you see that you could go on, adding your own examples? *The kingdom of heaven is like doing the dishes or the laundry? Paying the bills?*

Parables like these, and the ones Jesus tells, do not claim to give a complete and exhaustive account of anything. They are gestures pointing to what cannot be said.

I think Jesus is telling us that parable making should be a part of our life. We are not only to use our inherited ways of talking about God, from Scripture or the prayer book, but to find our own, our own new ways of saying what the kingdom is like, what God is like. The old ways are good, but we need new ways too, drawn from our own experience of life.

Jesus shows us how do this, for when he wants to explain what the kingdom of heaven is like he uses the materials from his own experience. In doing this he is showing us that God is present in the stuff of his ordinary life: in the yeast, the mustard seed, the treasure, the pearl, the fishing net. In the same way God is present in our ordinary lives too: in the sunset over the lake, in the baseball game, in the soufflé that rises perfectly (or doesn't), in the changing of diapers, in the settlement of quarrels among our kids, in the traffic jam, in the way passengers get on and off a bus, in the sleet and rain and the wind and the sun. God is in all our experience. That is why we can use that experience as the material of parables.

Jesus is telling us to look constantly for God's presence and power, his love and magnificence, in the most unlikely, unpretentious, ordinary places of life—to do, that is, just what he does.

For our lives take place in a world that is suffused with the presence and life of God, and we need to know it. God is not only in church but in the world. Jesus is saying something like this: "Look! Look! Open your eyes and ears and hearts, not just to my parables but to the stuff of parable in the world around you, to the presence of God in your own lives. Try it!"

Now I have to change focus a little, in order to face a perplexity that is, for me at least, presented by Jesus' interpretation of the parable about the fishnet. Do you remember it? He sees this story as an image of the last judgment, when evil people will be separated from the good, and thrown into the fire.

I have to say that I find this reading troubling. As I suggested earlier, I think it does not fit the actual life of the parable about the fishnet itself. I think it does not fit with the other parables Jesus has been telling, at least as I understand them. I think it does not fit with the whole meaning of Jesus' life and death and resurrection, which is a performance of amazing divine love.

My sense of the gospel passage as a whole is that it is telling us that if we are going to think or talk well about God, or the kingdom of God, we need to learn to engage in imagistic reasoning of the kind that Jesus demonstrates in these parables, with all its instability, inconsistency, obscurity, and openness to many meanings. When Jesus seems to violate that lesson himself, in his reading of the fishnet parable, and to do so in a way that does not seem loving, we face a real conundrum.

What can we say about it? Perhaps this is one of those places where Jesus is himself learning while he talks. Maybe his reading of the fishnet parable shows that he has not quite learned his own lesson. Maybe the troubling interpretation is an insertion by a later scribe or editor. Maybe this is a little examination in the reading of parables: Jesus hopes that we will have understood so well what he is doing that when he does this other thing, reducing the parable to an image of the last judgment, we will reject it and in this way affirm the real lesson he has been trying to teach us, about the nature of parables and their necessity in our lives. (I would like to believe in this solution, but I am not at all sure it works.)

I believe everything I have said about the earlier parables, but I also have the need or desire to find a way to live with the real perplexity that this passage presents. I cannot make this problem just go away by wishing it to do so. Nor can I confidently explain it away.

It is worth dwelling on this moment of real discomfort, because I do not think it is unique to me or to this passage. As you may have felt yourself, there are plenty of others like it in the gospels, where we come up against something we cannot quite understand or believe or accept. What should we do when that happens?

I do have one thought, really not mine but Paul's, to which I think we can turn whenever our understanding seems to fail us in the face of this sort of perplexity in the gospels. It is to turn away from the particular troublesome difficulty, the issue we simply cannot resolve, to something larger and more important: to what we know about Jesus and ourselves. Then perhaps we can say, with Paul, "I am convinced that neither death, nor life, nor angels, nor rulers, nor things present, nor things to come, nor powers, nor height, nor depth, nor anything else in all creation will be able to separate us from the love of God in Jesus Christ our Lord" (Rom 8:38).

AMEN

Questions

1. Can you think of some new ways to make parables like the ones Jesus tells? "The kingdom of heaven is like . . ."? Suppose you actually work out and write down two or three of these.

Does the set of parables you have made express a meaning beyond that of any one of the parables? Is the whole, that is, more than the sum of its parts?

How does this work? Do the parables you have composed interact with each other to create a new meaning? Or do they somehow define a space they do not fill, counting on the reader to fill them with his or her imagination?

2. Do you think that the fact that you can use ordinary experience and events in this way means, as I suggest, that God is present in everything around us? Is this activity, trying to make new parables, in fact a way for us to learn about God's presence? Look at one of your own parables with this question in mind.

3. As you know, I find the passage that speaks of the angels separating the good from the bad, and throwing the bad on the fire, very difficult indeed, and I propose no real solution to the problem. Does that say something about my own deficiencies of mind and spirit? About the nature of Scripture? About the world? How do you understand and respond to that passage?

4. If you were to make a prayer in response to the reading and work you have done in this chapter, what would it be?

15

Living Together in Unity

Again we have multiple readings, this time three of them. They all speak to the same theme, that of human beings living in unity. (Actually there are in a sense four readings, since it is the Psalm (133) that gives us our title: "How very good and pleasant it is when kindred live together in unity.") As you think about this language in connection with the passages from Scripture, ask what can be meant by the term *unity* and whether it is always a good thing. With whom do you yourself live in unity? How do you do so?

Genesis 45:1–15

Then Joseph could no longer control himself before all those who stood by him, and he cried out, "Send everyone away from me." So no one stayed with him when Joseph made himself known to his brothers. And he wept so loudly that the Egyptians heard it, and the household of Pharaoh heard it.

Joseph said to his brothers, "I am Joseph. Is my father still alive?" But his brothers could not answer him, so dismayed were they at his presence. Then Joseph said to his brothers, "Come closer to me." And they came closer. He said, "I am your brother, Joseph, whom you sold into Egypt.

"And now do not be distressed, or angry with yourselves, because you sold me here; for God sent me before you to preserve life. For the famine has been in the land these two years; and there are five more years in which there will be neither plowing nor harvest. God sent me before you to preserve for you a remnant on earth, and to keep alive for you many survivors.

"So it was not you who sent me here, but God; he has made me a father to Pharaoh, and lord of all his house and ruler over all the land of Egypt. Hurry and go up to my father and say to him, 'Thus says your son Joseph, God has made me lord of all Egypt; come down to me, do not delay. You shall settle in the land of Goshen, and you shall be near me, you and your children and your children's children, as well as your flocks, your herds, and all that you have. I will provide for you there—since there are five more years of famine to come—so that you and your household, and all that you have, will not come to poverty.'

"And now your eyes and the eyes of my brother Benjamin see that it is my own mouth that speaks to you. You must tell my father how greatly I am honored in Egypt, and all that you have seen. Hurry and bring my father down here."

Then he fell upon his brother Benjamin's neck and wept, while Benjamin wept upon his neck. And he kissed all his brothers and wept upon them; and after that his brothers talked with him.

Romans 11:1–2a, 29–32

I ask, then, has God rejected his people? By no means! I myself am an Israelite, a descendant of Abraham, a member of the tribe of Benjamin. God has not rejected his people whom he foreknew. Do you not know what the scripture says of Elijah, how he pleads with God against Israel? . . . For the gifts and the calling of God are irrevocable. Just as you were once disobedient to God but have now received mercy because of their disobedience, so they have now been disobedient in order that, by the mercy shown to you, they too may now receive mercy. For God has imprisoned all in disobedience so that he may be merciful to all.

The Gospel of Matthew 15:21–28

Jesus left that place and went away to the district of Tyre and Sidon. Just then a Canaanite woman from that region came out and started shouting, "Have mercy on me, Lord, Son of David; my daughter is tormented by a demon."

But he did not answer her at all. And his disciples came and urged him, saying, "Send her away, for she keeps shouting after us." He answered, "I was sent only to the lost sheep of the house of Israel."

But she came and knelt before him, saying, "Lord, help me." He answered, "It is not fair to take the children's food and throw it to the dogs." She said, "Yes, Lord, yet even the dogs eat the crumbs that fall from their masters' table."

Then Jesus answered her, "Woman, great is your faith! Let it be done for you as you wish." And her daughter was healed instantly.

The Church of the Mediator, August 14, 2011

May the words of my mouth and the meditations of my heart be always acceptable in thy sight, O Lord, my strength and my redeemer.

THE READINGS FOR TODAY seem to have a deep common theme, the idea captured in the language of Psalm 133: "How very good and pleasant it is when kindred live together in unity."

The question is how human beings can live together when they are divided by interest, feeling, and identity. This is in fact the central question of all social life: in the world, in America, in the church, and in our own branch of the church. How do we overcome the divisions that separate us?

This is certainly the issue in the passage from Genesis about Joseph and his brothers. You remember the story: the brothers first tried to kill Joseph by throwing him in a well, then decided to sell him into slavery when a caravan passed by. They took his bloodstained coat back to their father as proof that he had been killed by wild animals.

Now, years later, they have come to Egypt to seek food with which to survive a famine. They come before the most powerful man in Egypt, who turns out to be their brother Joseph. They are terrified. What will he do to them? Kill them? Sell them into slavery? Yikes.

In fact what Joseph does is to forgive them wholeheartedly. More than that: he releases them from their guilt, telling them not to be distressed or angry with themselves because they sold him. It was actually all part of God's plan: "God sent me before you to preserve life."

This is an amazing response by Joseph. Somehow he just puts away his anger and resentment, wholly justifiable as they are, and responds to the situation before him in love and hope. This is astonishing. Most of us surely would have felt at least some desire to make the brothers suffer for what they had done, but Joseph does not.

The result is that he and his brothers can live together in unity. He promises to settle them and their father in Egypt and to protect them. They embrace each other in love.

Here we are being told that one way to bring about a world in which "kindred live together in unity" is to practice deep and wholehearted forgiveness, as Jesus himself taught and showed us, on the cross and elsewhere.

The passage from Romans is also about kindred living together in unity. Paul is addressing Gentile Christians who feel that they are superior to Jews. Their reasoning is that the Jews represent the old covenant, which did not work out, mainly owing to their disobedience to God. The Gentile Christians, who are in the new covenant that was established by the death and resurrection of Jesus, thus feel highly superior to the Jews.

It is not entirely clear, but what Paul is saying is something like this: You Gentiles were once "disobedient" to God, in the sense that you were not in covenant with him; you have now received the mercy of being included in the covenant because of the "disobedience" of the Jews, namely their failure to live up to their covenant obligations; they are now "disobedient" in the sense that they are not part of the new covenant, but by virtue of the mercy you have received, they may in turn receive mercy themselves.

It is hard to follow the logic of all this, but the main point is clear: all of us have been disobedient, all of us receive mercy. No one is superior;

no one is inferior; we are in this together. We are all at fault, we are all blessed by the mercy of God. In this we are all the same. To recognize this essential fact may make it possible for kindred to live in unity.

The gospel passage brings us to face another kind of disunity, this one between the children of Israel and the Gentiles at the time of Jesus himself. For it was deep in Jewish culture that the Jews were the chosen people, set aside by God, superior to all others, especially to the Canaanites and Samaritans.

Thus it is that when a Canaanite woman comes to Jesus to ask him to release her daughter from the power of a demon, Jesus simply disregards her. He does not answer her at all. In a similar spirit, and maybe picking up a cue from him, the disciples say to Jesus, "Send her away, for she keeps shouting after us."

Jesus does recognize her humanity enough to explain his silence, but the terms in which he does so are remarkable. He says, "*I was sent only to the lost sheep of the house of Israel,*" as if this were an obvious and appropriate truth. She does not accept this rejection, but kneels before him, saying to him, "Lord, help me."

Jesus' response is simply jaw dropping: "*It is not fair to take the children's food and throw it to the dogs.*" Here he is flatly denying her full humanity and that of all the Canaanites, and doing so in the most vulgar and aggressive way: calling them dogs. He sounds like the worst kind of racist from the white South fifty years ago talking about African Americans. But I think the contempt he feels for her seems to him utterly normal, just as racist contempt usually does to the one who has it.

Faced with this humiliating rejection, she does not give up, but says, "Yes, Lord, yet even the dogs eat the crumbs that fall from their masters' table." At last Jesus can see and accept her humanity: "*Woman, great is your faith! Let it be done for you as you wish.*"

What are we to make of this? How can Jesus, of all people, Jesus the friend of sinners and outcasts of every kind, speak to her as he did? What is going on?

I think what is going on here is very familiar. We live with it every day. It is the desire to feel that the group we belong to—the caste, the race, the gender, the religion, the social class, the nation—is innately superior to another, to all others. We see it everywhere: in attitudes towards Christians of another ilk or Muslims or Jews or Mormons or people of a different race or people with a different language or accent or people just far away or in another country. When there is a war, which in some sense there always is, the humanity of a whole country or people is denied. This is what we do, and it is a deep sin.

It is obviously wrong and unjust for the Jews to consider the Canaanites dogs. But Jesus does it. How can it be that Jesus is guilty of this wrong? He is supposed to be perfectly good, perfectly without sin: can he really sin, as we do? Maybe the answer is that he is wholly man as well as wholly God, and that you cannot really be wholly human unless you participate to some degree in the dehumanization of others that marks your culture. Jesus is showing us, that is, how deep in our nature it is to think of others as dogs.

Of course he does not stop with that position but corrects it. This is something I love about this passage, one of my favorites in the whole Bible: it shows Jesus learning and changing. In this remarkable capacity for learning and change he is a model for us.

How could Jesus change and learn, you might wonder, if he was always perfect? Of course he had to change and learn if he were to grow from a baby into a man. One way we learn is through our mistakes, and this must have been one way he learned too.

But notice how and why he changes. He does not suddenly see, when he utters the word *dog*, that this is a terrible way to think about another person, especially a person suffering as the woman before him is. What brings about his change is the insistence of the woman on her own humanity and that of her daughter. She will not take "no" for an answer; she won't stop calling to him; she kneels before him; she shows how much she believes in his power; and then, at the critical moment, she meets his ugly language about dogs by turning it against him: even the dogs eat the crumbs from the table.

In a real way she is the hero of this story. Without her faith, her commitment, her insistence, Jesus would not have learned what he did. If he is a model of change, she is a model of faith.

So what are we to do with these three passages? The passage about Joseph tells us that pure and wholehearted forgiveness will help kindred live in unity. That is true. Paul's letter tells us to recognize that at the deepest level we are all flawed children of God and recipients of his mercy, and this will help us live in unity. That is true. The passage from Matthew tells us that we carry within us deep-dyed prejudices based not just on pride but on something even worse, the desire to think of others as dogs—to eliminate their humanity—and if we can heal ourselves of these prejudices, that will help us live in unity. That is true. The passages thus identify three forms of power that our society gives us—the powers of unforgiveness, pride, and contempt. If the kindred are to live in unity, we must give all these things up.

This all makes great good sense. But to give these things up may seem beyond us. They are part of our nature. We cannot recognize the humanity of all people, we cannot throw our pride out the window, and we cannot forgive as angels do. We just cannot. So says one voice within me.

But there is another voice that says that is both true and not true. We cannot do it perfectly, that is true. But we can do it more or less well, more or less imperfectly, and that is also true. We can take steps in that direction. We can do better than we have done. There are people like Nelson Mandela and Martin Luther King—both of whom simply and frankly and amazingly forgave their oppressors—who can show us the way.

In our efforts we are not alone. We have the help of Jesus: Jesus in the gospel, like this one, showing us how to change; Jesus in the church, this church, and in the Eucharist; and Jesus in our hearts.

We also have the help of each other, and of saints like the Canaanite woman, who stood up to the end for her child. Like her, we all have "children" too, actual or metaphorical: people we should never abandon, truths at the center of our hearts that we should never deny.

But we cannot be assured of success. Indeed we are certain to fail. So this is a moment for prayer, prayer that, in facing the responsibilities these three texts define, we may have some of the grace of Joseph, some of the wisdom of Paul, some of Jesus' capacity for responsive change, and some of the fiery strength of the Canaanite woman.

AMEN

Questions

1. Surely we all have experiences of living in disunity with our kindred, our friends, our colleagues, our fellow citizens. Think of one or two instances of such disunity in your own life, and ask how it might have been healed. What can we learn from Joseph, Paul, Jesus, and the Canaanite woman?

2. Are you troubled by the idea that Jesus could have internalized his culture's racist values to such a degree that he would act on them? Look at our own culture, and its racisms. How conscious do you think people are of thinking and acting in racist ways? How conscious are you yourself of these things?

3. It might be good to ask yourself also what other values you may have internalized without quite knowing it. Of course if the internalizations were unconscious you cannot easily identify these things, but the question is still a good one. We may have hints or intuitions about values we have never questioned. As you think about what these values are, ask yourself which of them you think you (and I and all of us) ought to reject? How is that rejection to be achieved? How are we to correct ourselves?

4. One way to think of what Jesus does in this passage is to say that he is teaching us how to correct ourselves. At first, Jesus is doing what we all do, all the time, namely, acting and speaking out of values we get from somewhere else, from the larger world or culture. But he corrects himself. How does he teach us to correct ourselves?

5. Turn again to the story about Joseph and his brothers. Why do you think Joseph was able to forgive his brothers? Is there a lesson here for us?

16

Suffering

The image that connects the first two readings given below is that of a vineyard which is at first fruitful, prosperous, and lovely, but is then (or will be) laid waste and destroyed. The desolation of the vineyard seems to represent the suffering that is, and always has been, such an endemic aspect of human life. In the third reading, from Matthew, we have the vineyard still, but this time it has been seized by the bad tenants, who, we are told, will surely be destroyed when the owner comes.

The question all three readings present is a crucial one: what relationship is there between such desolation, such suffering, and God?

Isaiah 5:1–7

Let me sing for my beloved my love-song concerning his vineyard: My beloved had a vineyard on a very fertile hill. He dug it and cleared it of stones, and planted it with choice vines; he built a watchtower in the midst of it, and hewed out a wine vat in it; he expected it to yield grapes, but it yielded wild grapes.

And now, inhabitants of Jerusalem and people of Judah, judge between me and my vineyard. What more was there to do for my vineyard that I have not done in it? When I expected it to yield grapes, why did it yield wild grapes?

And now I will tell you what I will do to my vineyard. I will remove its hedge, and it shall be devoured; I will break down its wall, and it shall be trampled down. I will make it a waste; it shall not be pruned or hoed, and it shall be overgrown with briers and thorns; I will also command the clouds that they rain no rain upon it.

For the vineyard of the Lord of hosts is the house of Israel, and the people of Judah are his pleasant planting; he expected justice, but saw bloodshed; righteousness, but heard a cry!

Psalm 80:8–19

You brought a vine out of Egypt;
> you drove out the nations and planted it.

You cleared the ground for it;
> it took deep root and filled the land.

The mountains were covered with its shade,
> the mighty cedars with its branches;

It sent out its branches to the sea,
> and its shoots to the River.

Why then have you broken down its walls,
> so that all who pass along the way pluck its fruit?

The boar from the forest ravages it,
> and all that move in the field feed on it.

Turn again, O God of hosts;
> look down from heaven, and see;

Have regard for this vine,
> the stock that your right hand planted.

They have burned it with fire, they have cut it down;
> may they perish at the rebuke of your countenance.

But let your hand be upon the one at your right hand,
> the one whom you made strong for yourself.

Then we will never turn back from you;
> give us life, and we will call on your name.

Restore us, O Lord God of hosts;
> let your face shine, that we may be saved.

The Gospel of Matthew 21:33–46

"Listen to another parable. There was a landowner who planted a vineyard, put a fence around it, dug a wine press in it, and built a watchtower. Then he leased it to tenants and went to another country. When the harvest time had come, he sent his slaves to the tenants to collect his produce. But the tenants seized his slaves and beat one, killed another, and stoned another.

"Again he sent other slaves, more than the first; and they treated them in the same way. Finally he sent his son to them, saying, 'They will respect my son.'

"But when the tenants saw the son, they said to themselves, 'This is the heir; come, let us kill him and get his inheritance.' So they seized him, threw him out of the vineyard, and killed him. Now when the owner of the vineyard comes, what will he do to those tenants?"

They said to him, "He will put those wretches to a miserable death, and lease the vineyard to other tenants who will give him the produce at the harvest time."

Jesus said to them, "Have you never read in the scriptures: 'The stone that the builders rejected has become the cornerstone; this was the Lord's doing, and it is amazing in our eyes'? Therefore I tell you, the kingdom of God will be taken away from you and given to a people that produces the fruits of the kingdom. The one who falls on this stone will be broken to pieces; and it will crush anyone on whom it falls."

When the chief priests and the Pharisees heard his parables, they realized that he was speaking about them. They wanted to arrest him, but they feared the crowds, because they regarded him as a prophet.

THE CHURCH OF THE INCARNATION, OCTOBER 2, 2011

May the words of my mouth and the meditations of my heart be always acceptable in thy sight, O Lord, my strength and my redeemer.

We all know that life can be very painful indeed: sometimes in expected ways, sometimes in ways we never dreamed of, sometimes just a little, sometimes beyond our endurance. But we all know that suffering itself is an indelible part of human life.

The question that today's readings raise is this: what relationship does God have with the suffering that is built into our lives? Where is God when destruction strikes?

We see one sort of answer in the Old Testament passages we heard today. We are told in Isaiah that God will tear up and destroy and utterly level the vineyard he has built, the vineyard he loves so much, the vineyard that is Israel. Similarly, the psalm says, in essence, "You brought a vine out of Egypt, you planted it, and it flourished, but now you have utterly destroyed it. The wild boars ravage it at will."

The way these texts imagine the relation of God to this destruction is clear: he causes it, and does so as a way of punishing Israel for its faithlessness or wrongdoing. Those in our own time who think this way imagine that the tornadoes and floods that came earlier this year are punishments for moral decay, the earthquakes a call to repentance, the collapse of our economy a well-deserved sanction for our departure from some way of right living.

But I think this way of imagining God, and his relation to our suffering, just won't work. For one thing, I don't think our God controls everything that happens in the world. There is too much evil that is richly rewarded, too much goodness that suffers terribly, for me to believe that. And the punishments talked about in Isaiah and the psalm are collective—punishments not just of wrongdoing individuals, or those without faith, but of their children and their grandchildren—and this seems deeply wrong. More simply, I just do not believe that our God is a punishing God. He is not that kind of father, but a father of a much better kind.

The image of God as the all-powerful judge, inflicting disaster on wrongdoers, is only one of many contrasting images of God in the Old Testament, where it was gradually given up. But it still has currency in many forms of Christianity, in the larger world, and sometimes in ourselves. Don't we on some occasions find ourselves thinking that suffering must be punishment for something we did? What are we doing when we feel that way?

We may be yearning for a simpler world than the one we have, a world with a coherent moral order ruled by an omnipotent God, a world in which we can make sense of suffering by seeing it as punishment for wrongdoing, punishment we can avoid by being righteous. This God is not a remote and isolated figure, paring his fingernails as he looks down on us, but engaged with us. He is in our lives. Better an authoritarian and abusive God than no God at all, we may think.

The trouble is that this way of thinking is not confirmed by our experience, especially where destruction and suffering are inflicted on the innocent, as so often happens. Plenty of human suffering is no one's fault, and by no stretch of the imagination fair.

We see this all the time. A child has leukemia or a blight of locusts destroys a crop or a plague like the influenza plague of 1919 kills millions of people or a car, going slowly, hits black ice and flips over, and the driver is killed.

We could go on and on. We shall all suffer, we have all suffered, greatly or in lesser ways. The whole Book of Job is about such things: afflictions, dreadful afflictions, suffered by a righteous man who has done nothing to deserve them. No one is at fault. Job's so-called friends, you remember, assume that all suffering is caused by God for moral fault on our part and that this must be true in Job's case. They reason back from the suffering and disaster that it must be a just punishment for *something*.

You can see why they want to do that, but it just won't work, either for Job or for us. We know that a baby who is born damaged cannot possibly have done anything to deserve it. There is lots of suffering in human life that is wholly undeserved. So where is God in all of this? If he is not the cause of our suffering, where is he when we suffer?

I think that God does have a real place in our suffering, though not as its cause; rather, as a presence in our hearts, loving and active, when it happens.

A friend of mine planned to retire a few years ago, and was eagerly looking forward to years of life with his beloved wife. But she unexpectedly got cancer and soon died. He was consumed with grief and anguish. Out of this experience he wrote a series of beautiful poems, about his wife and his own suffering at her loss, poems of real and permanent value. A few years later he met a woman who had lost her husband at about the same time. They gradually learned to trust and love again, and now have an extraordinary relationship, one that does not deny their respective griefs but builds on them. I think God has been at work in them.

A light shone in the darkness and the darkness comprehended it not.

Of course I don't mean that it was somehow just fine that his wife died, or that her loss was somehow made up for by the way he responded to it. Her death and his loss of her were utterly terrible. But it is still true that, faced with this terrible destruction and loss, and his own suffering, he found a way to live and love, and his new wife did too.

I think it is there, in the newness of life that can arise even out of suffering, not in the destruction that causes suffering, that we can find God.

Earlier this summer I went to a dreadfully sad funeral. A single mother had died in a car crash, leaving two young children behind her. In the sermon the priest said what we all felt, that this was simply awful, that this death made us feel that there was something deeply wrong in the structure of the world. In the face of this reality, our job, she said, was not to collapse in despair, but to take the broken pieces of life that lie around us and try to make them into something holy.

I think that God was present in those words, and that God is present, too, in the efforts that the family and friends are making to do what those words suggest.

What happens when we turn to the gospel passage and ask of it our question: "What is the relationship of God to human suffering and destruction?"

We see a very strange, a weird and seemingly inconsistent, almost kaleidoscopic combination of things. In the parable that Jesus tells, the tenants kill the messengers of the master; they even kill his son, for which, Jesus implies, they can expect to be killed themselves by the master (that is, by God). This is a world of murder, in which the tenants kill the messengers out of greed and the master is expected to kill the tenants out of his rage and sense of justice. In this sense it is completely continuous with Isaiah and the psalm.

But as I look longer at that scene, the story morphs in a dreamlike way into something very different indeed, in fact into its very opposite:

the image of Jesus on the Cross. In that image God is not a killer, even in just revenge, not a killer at all; he is the one who is killed. How can that be?

No longer is God saying, "Obey or be punished"; instead he is saying . . . what is he saying? What *does* the Cross mean? It seems impossible, almost crazy.

Jesus, as God's human presence on earth, channels all the violence and hatred in the world and directs it to himself. This is as far from the world of the Old Testament passages we heard today as one can well imagine.

Sometimes people say that Jesus is dying for our sins, paying the penalty for them as we could never do. But this does not make much sense, at least to me. That is really a continuation of the way of imagining God as punitive avenger demanding payment for wrongdoing.

Obviously I have no complete explanation of the mystery of the Cross, the central mystery of human history, but I do have some thoughts.

One is that Jesus is telling us that when we suffer we are not alone. He has been there, he has suffered, and does suffer with us. This means also that we need not be as strongly ruled as we now are by the fear of suffering, especially by the fear of what "they," our powerful enemies, may do to us. In many other places in the gospels Jesus says, "Do not be afraid," "Fear not," and he is saying that here too.

Something else, too: I think Jesus is telling us that when we ourselves are haunted by guilt or shame, and feel the corresponding human need, the compulsion, to inflict harm on ourselves or others, there is no need for us to do this, no need at all. It has already been done, once and for all. He is offering to break a cycle that leads to much suffering: the cycle of guilt or shame transformed into the desire to injure.

By his death, including his forgiveness of those who kill him, Jesus is offering to set us free from our own destructive and violent impulses, from our own desire to inflict suffering on ourselves and others, whether we do this by means of violence, or addiction, or humiliation.

In the freedom he gives us he is calling upon us to do what would otherwise be unimaginable: he calls on us to love our God with our whole hearts—how could we possibly not love such a God as this?—and to love our neighbors as ourselves.

AMEN

Questions

1. I have heard it argued, by very fine people, that punishment really is required for wrongdoing if we are to have any sense of shared and universal morality. If there are no adverse consequences, people will feel free to do whatever they want, however wrong or evil it may be. This is true, the argument goes, both in our own moral lives as individuals and citizens, where we should support the practice of just punishment, and theologically, in our conception of God, who should also be the source of just punishment.

What do you think of this line of argument?

2. Consider the question in connection with personal forgiveness, which the argument summarized above seems to oppose on moral grounds. Is it morally wrong to forgive? When it is right to forgive? What is forgiveness anyway?

3. What would happen to these arguments if we gave up the desire to judge others by a standard of right and wrong, leaving that to God, and focused instead on our own spiritual condition? This is what God means when he says, "Vengeance is mine." The idea is not that he delights in vengeance, but that we are not to act for him in inflicting it on other people. (See Deut 32:35; and Rom 12:19.)

4. To go back to our original question—what is the relation between God and human suffering?—do you think God causes it all, and does so for a reason?

5. This would be a good time simply to close this book and meditate upon Jesus on the Cross.

17

"Keep Awake"

The speech of Jesus we read today is a part of what is often called the Little Apocalypse, a portion of the Gospel of Mark in which Jesus looks forward to the end of time and to his own return in glory.

As you read it, ask what connection, if any, you can possibly imagine between this speech and your own life.

The Gospel of Mark 13:24–37

"But in those days, after that suffering, the sun will be darkened, and the moon will not give its light, and the stars will be falling from heaven, and the powers in the heavens will be shaken.

"Then they will see 'the Son of Man coming in clouds' with great power and glory. Then he will send out the angels, and gather his elect from the four winds, from the ends of the earth to the ends of heaven.

"From the fig tree learn its lesson: as soon as its branch becomes tender and puts forth its leaves, you know that summer is near. So also, when you see these things taking place, you know that he is near, at the very gates. Truly I tell you, this generation will not pass away until all these things have taken place. Heaven and earth will pass away, but my words will not pass away.

"But about that day or hour no one knows, neither the angels in heaven, nor the Son, but only the Father.

"Beware, keep alert; for you do not know when the time will come. It is like a man going on a journey, when he leaves home and puts his slaves in charge, each with his work, and commands the doorkeeper to be on the watch. Therefore, keep awake—for you do not know when the master of the house will come, in the evening, or at midnight, or at cockcrow, or at dawn, or else he may find you asleep when he comes suddenly.

"And what I say to you I say to all: Keep awake."

The Church of the Mediator, November 27, 2011

May the words of my mouth and the meditations of my heart be always acceptable in thy sight, O Lord, my strength and my redeemer.

THIS IS THE FIRST Sunday in Advent. When we hear Jesus' dramatic and mysterious speech about the Apocalypse we may well wonder what it has to do with this moment of the year. Let us see what happens when we try to establish some connections between this speech and the season it begins.

Today's Gospel is about time, and the end of time, which are difficult subjects to talk about, to put it mildly. In one sense time is totally familiar to us—we all have watches and schedules—but in another sense it is deeply strange.

Time is the medium in which we live, like a river. In the morning we have breakfast, then we set out on the day; we will never have that breakfast again, and we do not know what will have happened when the hour for breakfast comes around again tomorrow. The image of time as a river seems just right: at any one moment we are immediately and fully where we are in the course of the river, looking at the field of cows or the rocky cliff, but what lies around the bend we do not and cannot know. What we are seeing now we shall never see again, or not in the same way.

We greet one another when we come into church, and that moment is suddenly gone forever. We do not know when we shall greet each other next or what will have happened in the meanwhile.

That is microtime. We also live in macrotime, as we grow from babies into toddlers into kids into teenagers into adults and so on and on until we find that we are grandparents, beginning to be more fully aware that time, and life itself, will have an end for us. All the while everything is changing, within us and around us. I am no longer the fourteen-year-old boy I remember being, and the world in which that boy lived is gone forever.

This is how it is for us. It is very different for God, who lives outside of time, eternal and unchangeable. When he created the world, and living things, he created time too: time, within which the whole great adventure of life takes place. He can look at this adventure, and at time itself, from the outside, as we cannot.

But our Bible and our tradition tell us that he entered time—or perhaps I should say he enters time, since everything about him is in the present tense—in the form of his son Jesus, the Christ, a human being like us, who lived in time like us: growing from childhood to adulthood, learning to talk, experiencing hunger and thirst, making friends, traveling. These are all things we do too. He probably cut his knee, which took time to heal; he probably caught cold too. He had whiskers. He was fully human, and he died.

In today's Gospel, Jesus speaks about time, both from within it, like us, and from outside it, like the Father. He is *in time* in the most dramatic possible way: just two days from his death, his doom, and highly aware of the fact. He speaks out of that moment. But he is also in a sense *out of time*, for he is talking about the end of it all, the cataclysmic doom of the universe. Here he is imagining the whole world of time: time that began when God created the heavens and the earth and will end at some moment we cannot imagine, when the necessary conditions of life as we experience it no longer exist. But then he will come for us.

So what Jesus says here is weird and wonderful and frightening and reassuring all at once. This is true for us, as it must have been for the disciples too.

But we face a difficulty that the disciples were spared, namely, the fact that we know that Jesus' prediction, that this will happen during the lives of the present generation, does not come true. The end of time did not arrive in the lives of the disciples and has still not arrived, two thousand years later. Or is there a sense in which it has indeed arrived, without our knowing it?

That may seem a completely weird and impossible thought. How could we not know it if the end of time had arrived? So let me develop it a little.

In this passage Jesus seems to be speaking about something utterly unique, which will happen only once in history: the end of history itself. But I think that there is a way in which this image of doom is a part of our ordinary lives: we are always predicting doom, and we experience it. This is in fact a structural part of human life.

Sometimes we imagine a kind of cosmic doom looming over us. In every age people have felt that the world is in peril, and that it might well come to an end. We think about this today, and worry about it, and are right to do so. Think, for example, of the fear that global warming may destroy the world as we know it: flooding cities, destroying crops, turning forests into deserts, melting icecaps. It may already be responsible for the tornadoes and hurricanes and earthquakes that have become so common, and, whatever we do, we may not be able to stop its rapid progression. We feel that we are living with the real possibility of doomsday. It may actually happen, and perhaps before this generation passes away.

But this moment is not unique. If I think about the world in which I grew up, fifty or sixty years ago, it seemed then a real possibility that nuclear war with the Russians would destroy not only all people but all life on earth. It did not happen, but that does not mean it was not close. And how about World War II? The Great Depression? The flu epidemic? World War I? The Civil War? The slave trade? The near extinction of Native Americans? The religious wars in Europe? The Black Death? The fall of the Roman Empire?

I think we can go right back through all of history and discover that at nearly every stage there was in our collective consciousness a fear of impending doom. Not only that, this fear was often rational. We were often, maybe always, on the edge of total disaster.

We not only fear doom, we actually experience some of it in our ordinary lives. One important feature of the doom Jesus predicts is that everything will be changed, transformed beyond recognition. Some of this actually happens to us as a normal part of life—not at the cosmic level, of course, but still in a real way.

By the time you get to be my age you discover that the world has always been changing before your eyes, in ways you cannot understand and could not have predicted. These changes happen without our quite seeing them. We do not know exactly how it happened, but we do know we cannot go back to the world we knew as children. Everything is changed in a thousand ways: the way people move and talk, the relation between the city and the countryside, what we take for granted about our methods of communication, how we imagine our nation, what we take to be the purpose of life.

We experience the end of time in an even more obvious way when we die. We leave behind the world of time and change and enter a world we cannot begin to imagine or understand. And the end actually is coming, for you and for me: the end of our lives, perhaps in war, perhaps by accident, perhaps by disease, perhaps just as a result of weakness and age. But the end will come.

So how do we live with these facts: the sense that the world really is in peril; the sense that everything is changing in ways we cannot see or understand; and the sense that our own lives will come to an end, whatever that will mean? How does this passage speak to us as we face these issues?

I said before that God is outside time, not subject to its fluctuations and changes. He is eternally present. For him everything is in the present tense. This means that for him the creation of the world and the end of time, and everything in between, are always present. Thus Jesus is always being born, always being crucified, always in Resurrection. The "end of time" that Jesus predicts is not a onetime thing, but continually happening, a constant part of all our lives.

The world is deeply fallen, and falling further, but it has nonetheless the springs of life always within it. The end is always a beginning. Disaster comes, death comes, horrific cruelty and criminality come, but then comes the Lord, in our hearts, in our churches, in our friendships and loves, bringing new life.

To think this way may help us make sense of Jesus' advice to his disciples and to us: "*Keep awake.*"

Keep awake to the real peril the world is in; keep awake to our sense of incomprehensible change; keep awake to the certainty of our own death. Keep awake to something else, too, more important than anything else: the fact that, in every one of the end times that we experience, Jesus is always returning to us, a source of eternal love and light. He is coming to take us up from the four winds into a world of blessing and love.

So let us keep awake to the constant presence of Jesus in the world and in ourselves. In the birth of a new baby, for example, bringing the promise of a life of love and joy, and in much smaller signs of new life as well: the green shoots that show in a stream even in the wintertime, the sunset shot with color over the lake, the cheerfulness and warmth and pleasure with which we live together in this church, and the Eucharist we are about to share.

This is the first Sunday of Advent. What I think we learn from this gospel passage is that the Advent of Jesus is not a onetime thing but perpetual, always happening. It is not bound by history or time. So let us pray that we may keep awake to the thousands of ways Jesus is always coming into our lives, as a sacred presence in everything we do and know and experience.

AMEN

Questions

1. In this uncertain world, full of past and future destruction, in which the end may come at any time, Jesus urges his followers to "*Keep awake.*" This is his message not only to his friends but to everyone, to "all," that is, to us.

This is a frustrating commandment. What are we to keep awake to? How are we to keep from dozing off, or falling into insensibility? But it is also a wonderful one, which crosses the boundaries of time and culture with ease. There are whole traditions, like the Buddhist, that focus immense energy on the task of being "aware": aware of oneself, of the world, of other people. A life of awareness is a full life, the only full life. Jesus is saying something like that to us: be aware, keep awake.

This presents certain questions: How are we to be aware? Of what are we to be aware? How do we know whether we are aware? How would you begin to answer such questions?

2. Is part of Jesus' idea in making his injunction to *"Keep awake"* to move us in a direction we cannot quite comprehend, to a sort of newness of life that is truly new? Are we meant to be open to the miracle still to come? If so, does this make sense in the light of your own experience of life?

18

"The Kingdom of God Has Come Near"

This passage from early in Mark's Gospel tells several overlapping stories: Jesus' healing of Simon Peter's mother-in-law, his driving out of demons, his praying on a mountain, and his decision to set forth to "proclaim the message." As you read, ask yourself what these stories seem to have to do with one another. Pay attention also to the mysteries, the unknown things, beneath the surface—the mother-in-law's disease, the demons, the unknown prayer on the mountain—for these establish the conditions on which the stories are told, and they may have parallels in our own lives.

Where do you find yourself in this passage?

The Gospel of Mark 1:29–39

As soon as they left the synagogue, they entered the house of Simon and Andrew, with James and John. Now Simon's mother-in-law was in bed with a fever, and they told him about her at once. He came and took her by the hand and lifted her up. Then the fever left her, and she began to serve them.

That evening, at sundown, they brought to him all who were sick or possessed with demons. And the whole city was gathered around the door. And he cured many who were sick with various diseases, and cast out many demons; and he would not permit the demons to speak, because they knew him. In the morning, while it was still very dark, he got up and went out to a deserted place, and there he prayed. And Simon and his companions hunted for him. When they found him, they said to him, "Everyone is searching for you."

He answered, "Let us go on to the neighboring towns, so that I may proclaim the message there also; for that is what I came out to do." And he went throughout Galilee, proclaiming the message in their synagogues and casting out demons.

The Church of the Incarnation, February 5, 2012

May the words of my mouth and the meditations of my heart be always acceptable in thy sight, O Lord, my strength and my redeemer.

Today's reading from the Gospel of Mark may at first look like a rather random series of events: Jesus cures Peter's mother-in-law of a fever; he drives out some demons; he goes to a desert place to pray; and he says to his followers, "*Let us go on to the neighboring towns, so that I may proclaim the message there also.*" One thing follows another, but what do they add up to?

To understand this passage it may be helpful to think of what comes before it.

Mark has no infancy narrative, like Matthew and Luke, but begins his gospel with an account of John the Baptist, including his baptism of Jesus, followed by a brief mention of Jesus' Temptation in the desert. Then the story really begins: Jesus starts preaching, calls the fisherman as disciples, and teaches the Scriptures in Capernaum—"with authority, not as a scribe." There he also drives an unclean spirit from an afflicted man, a spirit that declares that Jesus is the "Holy One of God." When Jesus leaves the synagogue he goes straight to the house of Peter's mother-in-law, and our passage begins.

What I have summarized is very densely written, and a lot could be said about it, but the basic point is clear. Mark has been showing Jesus becoming more fully himself as he goes from one stage to another: baptism, preaching, calling disciples, teaching, and driving out unclean spirits. He has been discovering, and revealing, his powers and his identity.

In our passage this process continues. Let us see if we can discover the stages of Jesus' growth here.

The first stage is *healing*. Jesus cures Peter's mother-in-law of a fever, just as he cured the man in the synagogue. Here is a question that may sound odd, but I think it is important: what does it mean about the world Jesus inhabits that he engages in healing at all? The answer is obvious: it means that people need healing, which means that they are sick, which in turn means that the world is full of unmerited suffering. That is a fundamental truth about the way things were then, and still are. Mark makes no effort to explain it, or justify it. Neither does Jesus. It is one of the often unnoticed conditions of our existence.

In his acts of healing Jesus works against this fact of the world. He cannot make all the suffering go away, but he does what he can. In this he is teaching us two things: that evil is real and that it can be resisted, not just endured. He is teaching us an alternative form of life, a form of life I think he is himself discovering as he lives it.

Notice that when Peter's mother-in-law is healed she starts to serve Jesus and his friends. Her being healed enables her to serve. So when Jesus goes about healing people he is not just curing them of a biological ailment, like leprosy or a fever; he is changing them within themselves, enabling them to begin a new kind of life, the life he promises us. His healing does not just restore, it transforms.

Later that evening Jesus cures afflicted people by driving out demons, demons he does not permit to speak "because they know him." This is the second stage of Jesus' progress. It is *secrecy*.

Secrecy is a major theme in Mark. In the synagogue scene Jesus silenced the unclean spirit that was calling him the Holy One of God. In Mark's Gospel as a whole, Jesus repeatedly tells his disciples not to reveal who he really is. This is often called the "Messianic secret." Why does Jesus want to keep his identity a secret? Maybe partly for safety, but I think for another reason too, and one we share with him.

Do you ever have the feeling that something good, even something wonderful, is emerging in you that you cannot quite grasp? That you are being called to a life—to a pattern, a world, a self—that seems much, much better than what you now know, but which you cannot begin to express clearly even to yourself? The kind of thing I mean might be a mute stirring deep within you, tendrils of hope seeking the light. Maybe you feel it only in the watches of the night. Maybe you are afraid to admit it even to yourself, let alone go public with it. Maybe nothing comes of it.

If this is true of you, you are not alone. I think we all sometimes have the experience of an emerging self, a self we want to keep secret, a self too vulnerable, too little known even to ourselves, to be shared with the world. I think that Jesus may have been feeling something like this. He was discovering, little by little, a piece of the deepest truth about himself. Until he grasped this truth, and held it in his hand, it was a source of infinite vulnerability.

So he tells the demons and disciples alike, "Don't tell them who I am. I am not ready to be known and understood."

The first stage of Jesus' growth in this passage is *healing* and the second *secrecy*. The third stage is *prayer*.

At this crucial moment, Jesus goes to the deserted place to pray, alone. In his fear and uncertainty—as the healer, the transformer, the one who is known perhaps more fully to the demons than to himself—he is turning to the Source of all life, of all strength, of all truth. He takes his incomplete, unfinished, vulnerable self to the Unnamed One in prayer.

We do not know what Jesus said or did when he prayed. Did he use words, and, if so, what words? If not, how did he pray? He was alone in a deserted place in the dark. No one can tell us what he said or did. But as I imagine it, in Jesus' prayer there were no words. Not like the Book of Common Prayer. Just mutual silence in the dark: Jesus, naked in his soul, wholly present to the Source of all life and being, who was also wholly present, to him and with him.

I imagine Jesus prayed in this way until he discovered within himself a kind of deep clarification, until, that is, he knew more fully who he was and what he had come to do.

Can we learn to pray like that? To pray for the emergence of our true selves?

Nothing is more important. I saw an article the other day about what people said at the end of their lives. As usual in articles of this kind, they did not say they wished they had made more money or were famous or had traveled more or had won the gold ring of life. What they wished was that they had been more fully their real selves in what they said and did. They wished they had stood up for what they believed.

Jesus is showing us how to get there, namely, through prayer like his. From his prayer he discovers something new about who he is and what he is called to do. He may not know the whole thing, but he knows at least what ought to come next. "*Let us go on to the neighboring towns, so that I may proclaim the message there also.*"

This is a step on the long journey that will end at Jerusalem, on the Cross.

So we have *healing*, *secrecy*, and *prayer*. The fourth stage is *action*. Jesus leaves, with his friends, for the neighboring towns to "*proclaim the message*."

But what exactly does Jesus mean when he says he will "*proclaim the message*"? Will he explain who he is and where he comes from? Will he tell his followers how to live, giving them, as it were, a new law to replace the old? Will he expose the emptiness of the religious authorities, the brutality of the Roman Empire?

In the other gospels he does these things. But in Mark, except for some rather cryptic parables and some confrontations with the authorities in Jerusalem, he does not. His message is at once simple and mysterious: "*The kingdom of God has come near; repent and believe in the good news*" (e.g., Mark 1:15). Mark's Jesus does not offer us ideas or rules or principles or explanations or histories or theories or theological structures. Those are all things that other people created later to help us come to terms with him.

In Mark, Jesus is the divine presence in human form: infinite, incomprehensible, inexpressible. He burns like a supernatural flame with his own brilliant light. He goes from point to point on his path, transforming those he touches. He tells the world, "*The kingdom of God has come near; repent and believe in the good news.*"

Why does he not say "the kingdom of God is *here*?" Because it is not here, not completely here. The world is too full of suffering and sorrow. But it is near.

It is very near. It is always near, just around the corner, just beneath the surface of things. We see signs of it everywhere, in the laugh of a child, in the way the snow clings to the branch of a tree, in an act of courageous self-revelation—in our own inner stirrings, in the souls of people we love. It is the promise of new life, constantly breaking through to us.

So: *healing, secrecy, prayer, action.* Those are the stages by which Jesus grows into himself in this passage, one stage leading to another. The question for us is: can we make these stages our own?

Can we be healers in the world, maybe not of physical diseases, but of other things that need healing: sorrow, anger, dissension, addiction, inner destruction? Can we do this in a way that will help others become more than they were, more completely alive? In a way that helps *us* become more than we were, more fully alive?

Can we honor what must be kept quiet and secret in ourselves, and in others, what must grow first in secrecy and darkness before it comes into the light?

Can we pray in silence, present to the Holy One, listening at the core of the soul for what we are being told in our inner depths, and waiting for the clarification out of which we can act?

Can we move from prayer to action in the world, the world that has so much suffering, so much evil, the world that God has not yet made wholly his own but which he has truly come near?

Can we do these things? They may seem impossible; they *are* impossible. But we are called to try to do them with all our heart, and when we do try, we will find that we are not alone.

AMEN

Questions

1. Suppose you were to tell the story of your own life history, your own spiritual journey. It would naturally be a story of growth, increased

understanding, and new perception. Would it have stages like those we see in this part of Jesus' life: healing and secrecy and prayer and action? Other stages? What would they be?

It would be worth spending a substantial amount of time thinking about this, maybe even writing the story out. You might discover new connections between your experience and that of Jesus.

2. As you tell this story, you may remember yourself having life plans of various kinds: this is what you wanted to do when you were twenty or thirty or fifty, this is how you wanted to live, this is the direction in which you wanted to go, this is where you hoped to come out. What has happened to those plans?

As you think about these things, do you discover deeper patterns in your life, patterns of which you were unaware even while you were living them out?

What is the relation between plan and pattern? Did things work out exactly as you planned? Was it a collapse of your plan that made the pattern possible?

If the pattern was not the result of your plan, your conscious choice, where did it come from?

3. As Christians our task is to imitate Jesus. What would it mean to try to imitate the Jesus in this passage from Mark?

19

The Transfiguration of Jesus

The passage before us today is one in which the events of the gospel seem to have very little connection with ordinary life. As Mark tells it, Jesus is completely transfigured on the mountain (whatever that means), then he is joined by Moses and Elijah, with whom he talks. (About what?) Certainly this was an experience that eludes the capacity of Mark and the disciples to understand or express.

Do you have any experiences of what might be called transfiguration, in yourself or in others?

The Gospel of Mark 9:2–9

Six days later, Jesus took with him Peter and James and John, and led them up a high mountain apart, by themselves. And he was transfigured before them, and his clothes became dazzling white, such as no one on earth could bleach them. And there appeared to them Elijah with Moses, who were talking with Jesus.

Then Peter said to Jesus, "Rabbi, it is good for us to be here; let us make three dwellings, one for you, one for Moses, and one for Elijah." He did not know what to say, for they were terrified.

Then a cloud overshadowed them, and from the cloud there came a voice, "This is my Son, the Beloved; listen to him!" Suddenly when they looked around, they saw no one with them any more, but only Jesus.

As they were coming down the mountain, he ordered them to tell no one about what they had seen, until after the Son of Man had risen from the dead.

The Church of the Mediator, February 19, 2012

May the words of my mouth and the meditations of my heart be always acceptable in thy sight, O Lord, my strength and my redeemer.

The Transfiguration is an extraordinary story. Here are the three disciples on the mountaintop with Jesus when without warning he bursts into light, his clothes shining white; then, somehow, Moses and Elijah are there with him, talking with him. Peter, needing to do something, says let's build three huts, one for each of you. Then a voice from heaven says, "This is my Son, the Beloved; listen to him!"

What on earth is going on here? It has some of the fluid and unexpected and amazing character of a dream. It is wild.

Of course it is wild. It is a showing forth of God: God is bursting right through the forms of reality in which we normally live in order to reveal himself directly to us, both as Father and as Son. It is as though someone unzipped the ground and sky and we could see for a moment what is behind those familiar things, behind our familiar physical world, and it is the glory of God. This is not an experience most of us have had.

In fact we cannot really comprehend something like this. It is beyond nature, beyond the world we know. But it has antecedents in Scripture which may help us grasp it at least a little. The scene is plainly meant, for example, to remind us of God's "bursting through" to Moses on Sinai, smoking and burning in the night. This is the moment when God gave Moses the law for the people of Israel, in the stone tablets. When Moses came down from the mountain, his face was still glowing with light from the experience. This God is a mighty God.

Another antecedent, quite different in feeling, is God's revelation to Elijah, in the cave on the mountain. This time God was not in the great wind, not in the earthquake, not in the fire, but in what one translation calls "the sound of sheer silence." Equally breathtaking and mysterious.

In evoking these earlier "burstings through" of God, our passage is saying that Jesus is like Moses, the founder of Israel, and like Elijah, its restorer. It is God himself who implicitly says so, and says in addition, "This is my Son, the Beloved." This is a third "bursting through" of God.

Notice that in all three of these passages the revelation of God is not made to the whole world, but to a special person or group: Moses; Elijah; and here the three disciples, James, John, and Peter. These are all exclusive revelations, not universal ones.

There is another "bursting through of God" that happens earlier in the Gospel of Mark itself, at Jesus' baptism. Just as Jesus was coming out of the water, Mark tells us that the Spirit descended like a dove, and then "a voice came from heaven: 'You are my Son, the Beloved; with you I am well pleased.'"

In the Transfiguration we get a direct echo of this passage: "From the cloud there came a voice, 'This is my Son, the Beloved; listen to him!'" But notice this difference: in the first scene the voice speaks directly to Jesus, and only to him; in this one, the voice speaks to the disciples, in the first instance, and ultimately to the whole world, telling all of us who Jesus is. So in the end the revelation made in this scene will not be limited, as the others are, but universal, to everyone, to all time.

But not yet: Jesus tells his disciples to keep his identity a secret until *"the Son of Man has risen from the dead."*

These antecedents may help us see the Transfiguration passage as less strange and weird, but we may still want to ask, and rightly so: how does this burst of glory speak to us? What does this have to do with us? In particular, what does the voice mean when it tell us to "listen to him"?

This turns out to be a complicated question, for we are situated differently from the disciples. When they are told that they should "listen to him," they are being told to pay attention to what Jesus has already said to them, and will later say to them, face to face. But we did not know Jesus during his life on earth. He has not spoken to us face to face, as he did to the disciples, so how can we listen to him? He is no longer here.

I think this question occurred to Mark. It may even have been one of the complex set of things that led him to write his gospel, forty years after

Jesus died. Jesus had gone, and was not coming back soon. Mark saw that if people who had not been in Jesus' presence during his lifetime were to "listen to him," as the voice commanded, there must be a written record of what he said, a record they could read or hear. So Mark writes the gospel, as a way of telling the world who Jesus was, what he did, and what he said. This was the first gospel, and an astonishing, utterly original invention. There were no antecedents for this.

It is this gospel, and the others written after it, that give us the words of Jesus, the story of Jesus, to which we can listen, even now. It makes possible our lives as Christians. It has made possible the church itself.

There is another complication in this passage. After his Transfiguration, Jesus tells the disciples to keep quiet about the truth of his identity until after he has risen from the dead, when they can tell the world.

Why does Jesus want secrecy now, but not secrecy later? There are many possibilities, but one is this: if the "bursting through" of God that we have seen, of the Father and the Son, were truly known by the people, if it were known that Jesus was the Messiah, the whole story might blossom out of control. Jesus would be seen by many people as a future king, which could lead to armed insurrection, even against Jesus' wishes, and ultimately to almost certain military defeat. (Think of what happened in the year 70.)

But that is not the story Jesus came to live out, the story of a military leader who failed. Jesus' role is the opposite: to be the Holy One who dies voluntarily, not resisting, and who then returns to be with his friends. Jesus is not a figure of violence but of nonviolence, not a figure of human power but of powerlessness, not one who kills his enemies but one who loves and forgives them. He proclaims the kingdom of God.

For this to be his story, his secret must be confined to his disciples, if possible, until the moment comes when the tomb is found empty. Scholars tell us that in Mark's Gospel, as it was originally written, that moment at the tomb is where the story ends, with the man in white greeting the women and commanding them to tell the disciples that Jesus had risen and would meet them in Galilee. "But," Mark tells us, "they went away and told no one, for they were afraid."

That is the end. The End. There are no stories of the resurrected Jesus in Mark, no upstairs room with doubting Thomas, no broiled fish by the sea of Galilee, no supper in Emmaus. The story stops with the fear of the women.

A friend once suggested to me that this odd and fragmented ending is speaking to us, to us who may also be afraid like the women in the story, to us who may also want to keep our relation with Jesus a secret. It is telling us that it is up to us to finish the story. We are to say who Jesus is. We are to tell the disciples he is risen and will meet them in Galilee. We are not to be afraid. We are to proclaim his Resurrection to the world. More than that: we are to embody his Resurrection, by allowing him to live within us.

If we go back to the voice from heaven saying, "Listen to him," it is pretty clear what those words meant to the disciples. For Jesus was always telling them the same thing, one way or another: "Follow me." And he meant this literally: follow me on the journey to Jerusalem, to the Cross, to the Resurrection. Take up your cross and follow me.

This is not a set of moral rules, but the appeal of one person, Jesus, to other people, the disciples, calling them to follow him into a new life. This is a life no one can describe in words, but when it is found it will be the deepest and most immediate reality in the world.

We who are in this church today cannot "listen to" Jesus in exactly the same way as the disciples did, because we are not with him in Galilee in the year 30. We are in Harbert, Michigan, almost two thousand years later. We don't have memories of Jesus speaking to us in the flesh. But, thanks to Mark and the others, we do have the whole story of his life and death, including of course many of his words.

So we can listen to Jesus after all (though in a different way from the disciples), and we can follow him towards the same light and the same new life.

Today is the last Sunday before Lent. It is entirely right that we should be exposed to the display of divine glory on the mountain before the coming of the penitential darkness. It is also right that we should be told, as Mark's ending does, that it now depends on us, that we are asked, with the help of Christ and the grace of God, to complete the gospel, by realizing it in our own lives.

Thanks be to God.

AMEN

Questions

1. Have there been moments in your own life that seemed to involve an utter transformation of the natural world? Somehow the world was just not the same? Not all of us have had such an experience, but some people have. If that includes you, this would be a good time to recall and think about it.

2. Think now about the text we call the Gospel of Mark. Jesus died in about 30 C.E., and Mark's Gospel was written maybe thirty-five or forty years later. As I say in the sermon, I think the reason he wrote it was that he now saw that it was unlikely that Jesus would return as soon as he had expected and that the generation of people who knew him was dying off. The gospel was Mark's brilliant solution, a text that told Jesus' story, and kept his voice alive.

This was an invention by Mark. People sometimes speak of this gospel as though it were unsophisticated, a mere patching together of fragments from an oral tradition, but nothing could be further from the truth. (For one elaboration of this point, see Ched Myers, *Binding the Strong Man: A Political Reading of Mark's Story of Jesus*, 2008.) In my experience this gospel repays all the attention I can give it.

What was the original physical form of Mark's Gospel and how was it read by its early readers? Like most works in the ancient world it first existed almost certainly in the form of a scroll, which would be read not silently but aloud, usually in groups. Maybe the people present would take turns reading; almost certainly they would talk about the insights the gospel offered and the problems it raised. In this way the gospel stimulated conversation among believers, one in which we are still engaged—a conversation by which the community we call the church was initially formed and has been maintained ever since, including in what we are doing together in this book.

This is a long introduction to a short question: is Mark's Gospel itself a kind of Transfiguration?

20

Palm Sunday

The passages from Mark given below deal with two different events on two different days. The first is Jesus' entry into Jerusalem, triumphantly hailed by the crowd; the second, just days later, is the story of his Crucifixion, as bleak a drama as one could well imagine.

How are we to put these passages together? Or is part of their message that they cannot be put into a comprehensible pattern?

The Gospel of Mark 11:1–10, 15:1–39

When they were approaching Jerusalem, at Bethphage and Bethany, near the Mount of Olives, he sent two of his disciples and said to them, "Go into the village ahead of you, and immediately as you enter it, you will find tied there a colt that has never been ridden; untie it and bring it. If anyone says to you, 'Why are you doing this?' just say this, 'The Lord needs it and will send it back here immediately.'"

They went away and found a colt tied near a door, outside in the street. As they were untying it, some of the bystanders said to them, "What are you doing, untying the colt?" They told them what Jesus had said; and they allowed them to take it.

Then they brought the colt to Jesus and threw their cloaks on it; and he sat on it. Many people spread their cloaks on the road, and others spread leafy branches that they had cut in the fields. Then those who went ahead and those who followed were shouting,

"Hosanna!
Blessed is the one who comes in the name of the Lord!
Blessed is the coming kingdom of our ancestor David!
Hosanna in the highest heaven!"

As soon as it was morning, the chief priests held a consultation with the elders and scribes and the whole council. They bound Jesus, led him away, and handed him over to Pilate.

Pilate asked him, "Are you the King of the Jews?" He answered him, "You say so." Then the chief priests accused him of many things. Pilate asked him again, "Have you no answer? See how many charges they bring against you." But Jesus made no further reply, so that Pilate was amazed.

Now at the festival he used to release a prisoner for them, anyone for whom they asked. Now a man called Barabbas was in prison with the rebels who had committed murder during the insurrection.

So the crowd came and began to ask Pilate to do for them according to his custom. Then he answered them, "Do you want me to release for you the King of the Jews?" For he realized that it was out of jealousy that the chief priests had handed him over. But the chief priests stirred up the crowd to have him release Barabbas for them instead.

Pilate spoke to them again, "Then what do you wish me to do with the man you call the King of the Jews?" They shouted back, "Crucify him!" Pilate asked them, "Why, what evil has he done?" But they shouted all the more, "Crucify him!" So Pilate, wishing to satisfy the crowd, released Barabbas for them; and after flogging Jesus, he handed him over to be crucified.

Then the soldiers led him into the courtyard of the palace (that is, the governor's headquarters); and they called together the whole cohort. And they clothed him in a purple cloak; and after twisting some thorns into a crown, they put it on him. And they began saluting him, "Hail, King of the Jews!" They struck his head with a reed, spat upon him, and knelt down in homage to him. After mocking him, they stripped him of the purple cloak and put his own clothes on him. Then they led him out to crucify him.

They compelled a passer-by, who was coming in from the country, to carry his cross; it was Simon of Cyrene, the father of Alexander and Rufus.

Then they brought Jesus to the place called Golgotha (which means the place of a skull). And they offered him wine mixed with myrrh; but he did not take it. And they crucified him, and divided his clothes among them, casting lots to decide what each should take.

It was nine o'clock in the morning when they crucified him. The inscription of the charge against him read, "The King of the Jews." And with him they crucified two bandits, one on his right and one on his left. Those who passed by derided him, shaking their heads and saying, "Aha! You who would destroy the temple and build it in three days, save yourself, and come down from the cross!" In the same way the chief priests, along with the scribes, were also mocking him among themselves and saying, "He saved others; he cannot save himself. Let the Messiah, the King of Israel, come down from the cross now, so that we may see and believe." Those who were crucified with him also taunted him.

When it was noon, darkness came over the whole land until three in the afternoon. At three o'clock Jesus cried out with a loud voice, "Eloi, Eloi, lema sabachthani?" which means, "My God, my God, why have you forsaken me?" When some of the bystanders heard it, they said, "Listen, he is calling for Elijah." And someone ran, filled a sponge with sour wine, put it on a stick, and gave it to him to drink, saying, "Wait, let us see whether Elijah will come to take him down."

Then Jesus gave a loud cry and breathed his last. And the curtain of the temple was torn in two, from top to bottom. Now when the centurion, who stood facing him, saw that in this way he breathed his last, he said, "Truly this man was God's Son!"

The Church of the Mediator, April 1, 2012

May the words of my mouth and the meditations of my heart be always acceptable in thy sight, O Lord, my strength and my redeemer.

Today's gospel readings make an almost impossible pair. First we heard about Jesus' triumphant entry into Jerusalem, when the people hail him as the one who will restore the kingdom of David. Second, we just acted out right here, in a kind of reader's theater, the horrible caricature of a trial, ending in Jesus' death by torture on the Cross. One story is of joy and celebration, the other of immeasurable grief and sorrow.

What does each of these powerful stories mean, standing alone, and, much harder, what do they mean together? What is the truth of them? How are we to think about these things?

I want to start with a rather simple and obvious point, which is that the bare facts of these stories, like the facts of any story, mean different things to different people.

Take the death of Jesus. To Pilate, it means the end of a possible rebellion and, as a bonus, better relations with the Temple authorities. To those authorities, it eliminates a threat to their power as collaborators with the Empire. To the crowd that welcomed him into the city, it means the destruction of their hopes for a new king of Israel. To the crowd that calls for his crucifixion, its meaning is not entirely clear to me, but it has something to do with the need to make someone a scapegoat. To the men with him on the cross, it gives them a chance to taunt a man who claimed to be more powerful than they, but now seems to be no such thing. To the disciples, who abandoned him, it means the loss of their deep but unarticulated hopes—in some way mistaken hopes—for what they thought Jesus offered them. To the women, it perhaps is just another example of male destructiveness, leaving them as usual to pick up the pieces in grief.

So when we look at these events—Jesus' arrival in Jerusalem, his death on a cross—it is not enough just to recite facts, for the facts alone do not yield reliable meanings. There are multiple meanings, which are often expressed in formulations that prove to be false.

Think of the triumphant procession into town: "Blessed is the coming kingdom of our ancestor David!" Actually the crowd has it wrong.

Jesus is not coming as a future king, a military leader who will reestablish the autonomy of Israel. Not at all. He is coming to save them, but in ways they cannot imagine. He has no interest at all in political or military power. Their story misses the point.

Pilate's version of the story, that Jesus claims to be King of the Jews and thus commits treason against the emperor, also misses the point. Jesus never wanted to be that kind of king, and the peace Pilate thinks he is buying will be very short-lived at best. The crowd calling for his crucifixion misses the point too. They see in his death the satisfaction of some deep violent need—but we know it will not be satisfied, because it never is. The soldiers are likewise clearly wrong when see him as the object of their sadistic play; so, too, are those crucified with him when they see him as the proper object of their taunts: "He saved others, but he cannot save himself."

When Jesus cries out to God, "Eloi, Eloi,"—which in Aramaic means "My God, my God,"—the bystanders do not understand him, and think he is calling for Elijah. No one seems to understand him at all. People not only think different things; they think wrong things.

As for us, here is a bitter truth. If we had been present we might have been in any of those human roles, uttering false claims of meaning: in the Palm Sunday crowd, in Pilate, in the crowd shouting "Crucify him!," in the soldiers, in the others on their crosses, in the disciples offstage who feel abandoned, in the people who do not understand what Jesus means when he says "Eloi, Eloi." In each case we would think we see Jesus but we would not.

I think that Mark has written this passage very carefully in such a way as to make plain to us two points: first, the facts alone will not tell us their meaning; and second, in our efforts to give the facts shape and meaning we are constantly tempted to find and state false meanings, meanings driven by our own perspectives, our own desires, our own mentalities.

For Mark there is clearly an immense gap between all these false meanings and the true meaning of Jesus' entry into Jerusalem and his death on the Cross. But exactly what is that true meaning? Mark does not answer this question. In fact it appears that for him the truth of Jesus is humanly incomprehensible. No one gets it, not even his friends and followers. Whatever they say, they cannot grasp him. He is beyond the grasp of our minds. This is Mark's third point.

The incomprehensibility of Jesus has in fact been a major theme of Mark's Gospel from the beginning. Over and over again the disciples themselves show that they do not understand him. Even when Peter declares that he is the Messiah, and Jesus confirms that that is (in some sense) true, this knowledge quickly disappears from their minds.

The meaning of Jesus' life and death is likewise not manageable by us today. It is beyond our intellectual and imaginative power. Every effort we make to claim that it means this or that is doomed to failure, one way or another. After all, we are talking about God, and of course he is beyond us.

But when we read these stories we want to give them meaning. We need to do that. What do we do with this desire? What can we say? What help does Mark give us?

As you may have been thinking all along, there is one person who really does seem to speak the truth, the centurion: "Truly this man was God's Son." Mark also uses a similar phrase at the very beginning of his gospel, when the voice speaks from heaven at Jesus' baptism. These statements, at the beginning and end, clearly do state what Mark believes to be the core truth about Jesus. They frame the gospel, like bookends.

But what does the phrase "Son of God" actually mean? It is only a phrase, after all. Mark never explains what he thinks it means. Similarly, he does not set forth a set of things we should believe about Jesus, as if he were a theologian writing a creed—nothing about Virgin birth, for example. Rather, he offers us the experience of Jesus himself, talking and acting in his often mysterious ways.

Mark refuses to meet our need for formulations and explanations with which we might manage the unmanageable, and in doing so he teaches us something important. We want a kind of certainty, a set of take-away formulations, but we are not to have them. Mark does not give us theology. His aim is not to tell us things, but to give us an experience—the experience of Jesus going like a blazing flame through the world and transforming everything he touches.

The truth of Jesus, the truth of these stories, is not an idea or a proposition, but the experience of a person. This is Mark's fourth point.

Of course it makes sense that this person—Jesus, the Son of God—is beyond our understanding and imaginative control. But here I can't help thinking about us too. Are we also beyond understanding, beyond formulations, beyond our own imaginative control?

I may be speaking only for myself here, but I think there is a part of us, a deep part, that is actually not understood by others, not ever. We do not understand this part in other people either. There is a sense in which we do not understand it in ourselves. It is deeply mysterious.

Of course we often think we understand other people, but do we really and fully? To test this out we might ask ourselves who we do really and fully understand. Our parents? Our children? Our spouses? Our friends? And who really and fully understands us?

I think there is something not only in Jesus but in everyone that by its nature we cannot ever understand, no matter how well we come to know him or her, something in each of us that is never understood. The teenager who says to his parents, "You do not understand me and never have!" is speaking truly for this side of the self, dramatically and loudly.

The part of us that cannot be understood is not a set of quirks or foibles, but the core: the spring of newness, of creation, of fresh life within us, the very center of the self. This principle of new life cannot be understood, cannot be reduced to a formula, cannot be predicted, cannot be defined by external conduct, past or present, but is a mysterious source of new meaning. It is what enables us to surprise each other. It is the center of our selves. It is what makes each of us a person. It is our soul.

It is the presence of God within us, the presence of Christ.

We see this in the newborn baby, who is always a unique center of meaning and life. She has never been here before, and now she is. She is of infinite importance. She can never be completely known. She can only be experienced, as a person, as Jesus was.

The incomprehensible Jesus is not just there in the past, but lives on in the gospel text, lives on within each of us, at that central core of mysterious life. He is the flame of new meaning within us, blessing, encouraging, guiding. They could not kill him after all.

It is our task to recognize this spring of new meaning within ourselves, and within all other people too, to live out of it, to speak out of it, to express it and respond to it, and in this way to become the people of

Christ, not in a concept, not in a formula of theology, but in our deepest selves, alone and together.

AMEN

Questions

1. The two passages from Mark's Gospel seem to call for opposite feelings: triumph and joy at Jesus' entry into the city, grief and sorrow at his death. But are these the feelings you actually have as you read, or are they more mixed, with a foreboding that tempers the joy, with a recognition of Christ's life and power that tempers the grief? This combination of opposites may express a deep truth of human life, that both things are always with us. This may in fact be part of the point of the Christian story of death and resurrection.

2. It seems to be an essential element of Jesus' life that no one really understands him, not ever. I have suggested in the sermon that this is actually a feature of all human life. Is this right?

   Think of your own experience: who fully understands you? Do you fully understand yourself? I think probably not. But perhaps sometimes we have the *feeling* of being understood, or if that is not quite right, a feeling of belonging that is so strong that it does not matter that we are not "understood." Does that correspond with your experience? What is happening on these occasions?

3. What do you feel when you are most aware of the presence of God? Understood? Loved?

4. In Mark's Gospel we see lots of different people using formulations to express Jesus' identity, all of which are wrong or, in the case of the centurion, highly incomplete. Can you think of erroneous formulations that have been used about you? That you have used about other people? That you have used about God, or Jesus? Now the hard question: what would be good ways to talk about God, or Jesus—or you?

21

"Love One Another as I Have Loved You."

The commandment Jesus gives his friends in this speech at the end of his life is to love one another as he has loved them. In the view of many people, certainly John the Evangelist, this is the core of what Jesus stands for and means. But what can this commandment actually mean for us? What does Jesus mean by "love"? How can he *command* it? (Is love something that can be compelled?)

The Gospel of John 15:9–17

"As the Father has loved me, so I have loved you; abide in my love. If you keep my commandments, you will abide in my love, just as I have kept my Father's commandments and abide in his love. I have said these things to you so that my joy may be in you, and that your joy may be complete.

"This is my commandment, that you love one another as I have loved you. No one has greater love than this, to lay down one's life for one's friends. You are my friends if you do what I command you.

"I do not call you servants any longer, because the servant does not know what the master is doing; but I have called you friends, because I have made known to you everything that I have heard from my Father. You did not choose me but I chose you. And I appointed you to go and bear fruit, fruit that will last, so that the Father will give you whatever you ask him in my name. I am giving you these commands so that you may love one another."

The Church of the Mediator, May 13, 2012

May the words of my mouth and the meditations of my heart be always acceptable in thy sight, O Lord, my strength and my redeemer.

Today's gospel contains part of Jesus' long speech to his disciples before they go to the garden of Gethsemane, where he will be arrested. Like the whole speech, what we just heard is hauntingly beautiful, like a song or musical meditation. It is highly repetitive, circling through the same images and ideas in an intoxicating and somewhat disorienting way, always in the service of the same message. I think this is a way in which Jesus is recognizing that what he wants to say cannot quite be said in human language. At the same time it is paradoxically a way of expressing a deep and urgent desire to be understood.

The message is that as the Father loves him, so Jesus loves his friends; so, too, are his friends to love each other. Love is at the center of it all, especially of the community he leaves behind him—the community that will become the church, including this church, the Church of the Mediator.

This is beautiful beyond words. We feel in the presence of Jesus' love, and who wants to be anywhere else? But it has certain difficulties, at least for me—difficulties that I think turn out in the end to be gifts and blessings, in part because they are deep challenges to a way we often like to think of ourselves and our lives.

Difficulty one: Jesus tells his disciples, "*You did not choose me but I chose you.*" This was literally true for the disciples, who were called by Jesus in person, but it is also meant to be true of us. He is telling us that we did not choose him; he chose us.

This may seem an odd thing to worry about. But my lawyer's mind goes to work, and asks what if he did not choose us? What then? Could we still choose him? What is more, as his speech makes clear, what he is choosing us *for* is a commandment we cannot possibly obey, namely, to love one another as he loves us. So when I hear him say that he chose us, we did not choose him, I feel a challenge to my own sense of autonomy. The most important thing in life is not in our control but his control.

This is something that a certain side of me, and I think maybe a side of you too, does not want to hear. It is inconsistent with the image of ourselves as competent adults, out of which we live almost all the time.

According to this image we move through the world making our own choices: choosing where we live, what we do for a living, whom we marry, how we entertain ourselves, what presents we buy others for Christmas or birthdays, what we eat for dinner or breakfast, how fast we walk, whether we take the bus or the train. Everything. Absolutely everything. Our life is what we make it. We are the choosers.

But is that really how life works? We think we choose freely and competently, but do we really?

As I have thought about this, I have found myself wondering, for example, where the values on which we base our choices actually come from. Do we just fashion them ourselves in an internal workshop of some kind? Or do we choose them from some array presented by the world? I think in fact we often internalize the values created in our culture, sometimes including dreadful values, without even knowing it. To that extent, our choices of value are not wholly our own, not wholly free.

Even Jesus did this, if you remember the story of the Canaanite woman. She wanted Jesus to heal her daughter, and he refused, saying that he had come for the children of Israel, not for Canaanites, adding, "*It is not fair to take the children's food and throw it to the dogs.*" Jesus was calling this woman a dog! He had internalized the ugly racism that was part of his culture. He corrected it quickly, but this value of his culture had become a part of him.

To take another example, a white child growing up in the South before the Civil War would almost certainly have internalized the view that African Americans are less than fully human, even if his own personal experience was inconsistent with that. As he grew up in the world, perhaps as a slave owner, the internalization would become deeper and deeper, until he was making horrible decisions and choices on that basis—decisions and choices he thought of as his own, as good and natural, but which were really those of the culture at large.

How about us? What values have we internalized? It is a disturbing truth that we really cannot know the answer to that immensely important question. Like Jesus and the slave owner, we are almost certainly unaware of the values, good or bad, that have seeped into us from our larger world. They seem utterly natural.

But racism is part of us, for sure. We certainly do not recognize the full humanity of others in our country and around the world, we are unavoidably affected by the empty images of human happiness we see in TV ads, and we are stimulated by political arguments to think in simplistic and sentimental ways. These are not good things.

We are partly the creatures of our culture, for good or ill, without knowing exactly how. So the image we have of ourselves as consciously choosing our values and competently making decisions on that basis is not really true.

When we think about how our life choices actually work out, there is even less reason to be confident in our capacity to choose. When we make important choices, we often have no real idea what they will actually mean.

Suppose we decide to move to St. Louis, where we have an exciting job offer. What will life in St. Louis be like for us? What will the job be like? We cannot know. Suppose we meet someone there and fall in love and get married. Did we choose that? In what sense?

We decide to have children. Here we cannot possibly know what we are doing. When our first baby is born our whole world will be different, from the inside out, in ways we cannot imagine ahead of time. In one way we chose to have a baby, but we certainly did not know what we were doing, because no one does. Life is an adventure undertaken largely in ignorance of ourselves, our culture, and the world.

It is important to recognize that there can be a kind of amazing blessing here: notwithstanding our ignorance about where our values come from, and about what our choices mean, our lives can turn out to have deep meaning of a surprising kind. When we are old, looking back on life, we may see shapes in our lives that we could not see before. We may the see that things we really did not want to happen—a broken engagement, the loss of a job, ill health, a failure in school, a nervous breakdown—were in fact good for us, and that some of our apparent successes, like a promotion, for example, or a professional honor, were not good for us at all.

Maybe when this happens we are beginning to look at our lives with God's eyes, God's values, not our own. It is certainly not the result of our competent and autonomous choices.

The image of ourselves that Jesus is challenging—the image that we are independent and competent choosers acting out of our own values—turns out not to be true. Jesus is asking us to accept that we can be the chosen, not the chooser, that we do not know all we think we know, that even our values are not completely our own, that we need help. He is breaking down our misconceived image of ourselves. He is rescuing us from ourselves. It is a blessing.

The truth is, we are not in control of our values or our lives. We need to be chosen. Our choices are never enough to rest our lives on. To live with that truth is to make it possible to begin to live another way, with trust, as Jesus would have us live: trust in life, trust in our true selves, trust in God.

The second difficulty in the passage arises from something I mentioned earlier, Jesus' central commandment to his followers: that they should love one another as he has loved them.

This is beautiful and wonderful, but it has a problem, once more a problem of our incapacity: we simply cannot love each other as he loves us. He is the Son of God, the Light of the World; his very essence is love. We are fallible and broken human beings, whose every action and feeling is touched with selfishness. He is commanding us to do what we cannot do.

We might ask: why does Jesus give us this impossible command instead of what we might call a "workable program" or a set of rules we can actually follow? The reason is that he is not interested in having us follow rules. Jesus is asking from us not obedience but love, and not just any love—not selfish or sentimental love, certainly not the abuse that often masquerades as love—but love like his, love that truly puts the other person first.

He knows he is asking us to love beyond our power to love. He is asking us to recognize what we can and cannot do, and to live on those terms.

Indeed I think the impossibility of the command is part of its point, an explicit recognition of the truth of our incapacity. This is what enables it to work as a deep challenge to our self-image of autonomy. In this it is like his insistence that we did not choose him, he chose us. The impossibility of his commandment is itself a blessing. It is an invocation of truth.

Jesus is asking us to put aside the part of the self that works by reason, calculation, and decision, and to dwell in the part that trusts, the part that can live with its own desire for the impossible and the ideal, the part that can begin to inhabit the world of love that he promises. Jesus is challenging the first part of the self, the side that claims autonomy and competence, in order to call into fuller being the second part, the part that is capable of love and trust. He is calling into being our naked souls.

When he tells us to love one another as he loves us, he is saying that we should take his love as a model for our own. We are to love like *that*, putting the other person at the center, not ourselves, loving our neighbor as ourselves. We cannot do this perfectly, but we can move in this direction. We can orient ourselves towards this sun rising in the east, and Jesus tells us why: because he has loved us.

This is not surprising. We all learn to love from being loved by others. We learn to trust by being trusted by others. The child who grows up loved and trusted by her parents will be naturally capable of love and trust; the one who is not will have a much harder time doing these things.

Jesus himself tells us that he was loved by the Father, and suggests that this is in fact why he can love his disciples, and us too, as he does. We are loved by him, in the way he loves; this is why we can begin to love each other, in the way he has shown us to love. In the world Jesus is creating, this is what it means to be chosen.

AMEN

Questions

1. As you think about your own life, can you see times in it when your image of yourself as an autonomous and competent person broke down, when you made plans and strove to achieve them and were disappointed in your efforts, but later discovered that this disappointment was actually good for you? That what actually happened gave a

shape or design or pattern to your life that was inconsistent with your plan? Better than your plan?

Do you find, that is, that you have been living out a story that has a shape and meaning very different from anything you had intended? How do you explain, or even talk about, such a matter? *"You did not choose me but I chose you."*

2. Do you have a sense of what might be called your primary or fundamental values, on the basis of which you make your life decisions? Where did those values come from, and to what extent are they really yours? Are you confident that these values are in fact the grounds of your decisions? Or have you internalized other values, without quite knowing it, values that would not bear the light of day? If you are uncertain on these matters, what should you do about your uncertainty?

3. Jesus asks us to love God with all our hearts and to love our neighbors as ourselves. None of us can do these things perfectly or even well. How do you live with the impossibility of what he asks?

22

Jesus' Healing

This passage from Mark captures some of the chaos of Jesus' life. A huge crowd comes to him; his family tries to get him to come inside, for he is being called crazy; the scribes sent from Jerusalem accuse Jesus of being the devil's agent, driving out demons by the power of demons; in response he says that they are sinning against the Holy Ghost, the unforgiveable sin. When he is told that his mother and sisters and brothers are calling him, he says, "*Who are my mother and sisters and brothers?*"

How are we to begin to make sense of such a passage?

The Gospel of Mark 3:20–35

And the crowd came together again, so that they could not even eat. When his family heard it, they went out to restrain him, for people were saying, "He has gone out of his mind."

And the scribes who came down from Jerusalem said, "He has Beelzebul [a name for the spirit of evil], and by the ruler of the demons he casts out demons."

And he called them to him, and spoke to them in parables, "How can Satan cast out Satan? If a kingdom is divided against itself, that kingdom cannot stand. And if a house is divided against itself, that house will not be able to stand. And if Satan has risen up against himself and is divided, he cannot stand, but his end has come. But no one can enter a strong man's house and plunder his property without first tying up the strong man; then indeed the house can be plundered.

"Truly I tell you, people will be forgiven for their sins and whatever blasphemies they utter; but whoever blasphemes against the Holy Spirit can never have forgiveness, but is guilty of an eternal sin"—for they had said, "He has an unclean spirit."

Then his mother and his brothers came; and standing outside, they sent to him and called him. A crowd was sitting around him; and they said to him, "Your mother and your brothers and sisters are outside, asking for you." And he replied, "Who are my mother and my brothers?" And looking at those who sat around him, he said, "Here are my mother and my brothers! Whoever does the will of God is my brother and sister and mother."

The Church of the Incarnation, June 10, 2012

May the words of my mouth and the meditations of my heart be always acceptable in thy sight, O Lord, my strength and my redeemer.

In the passage we just heard, Jesus is early in his ministry in Galilee. So far he has mainly been a healer; he has healed a man with an unclean spirit, a paralyzed man, a leper, and numberless others suffering from disease.

Today I want to talk about three things: his healing, his disturbing mention of the unforgiveable sin against the Holy Spirit, and how we can connect these issues to our own lives.

About Jesus' healing: the scribes—who were political operatives sent from Jerusalem to deal with this itinerant preacher and medicine man—have their own idea on this subject, namely, that Jesus is acting as a servant of evil: "by the ruler of the demons he casts out demons."

This is a complex moment. Let us begin by thinking about the unclean spirits or demons Jesus drives away. What or who are they?

In the gospels they are sometimes physical diseases, like leprosy, blindness, or paralysis; sometimes they are disturbances of another kind, mental or emotional or spiritual; sometimes they are both at once. I think that we are to regard these afflictions as completely real. The individuals who suffer them truly suffer, sometimes hideously so. But I also think that these people serve as images or metaphors for the human condition, a condition we share, for we too are afflicted with demons, with injuries to our souls.

What are the demons or unclean spirits in our own lives, the impairments of our inner selves? One small but significant demon many of us may know about firsthand is addiction to smoking. We know smoking is not good for us. It does not give lasting or real pleasure; in fact it makes us feel bad. But, based on my own experience at least, it is something we find very difficult or impossible to stop doing. It is like being possessed or inhabited by an enemy we cannot defeat.

Much the same is true, I would think, of other addictions, whether to material substances like alcohol or drugs or to obsessive or compulsive patterns of feeling and conduct, like unhealthy eating patterns or filling our houses with junk or constantly washing our hands. In some sense we want to stop what we are doing, we want to be free, but we cannot make that happen. The demon has become part of us.

Other kinds of demons work in much the same way. Think of a person who is full of obsessive hatred for a boss or coworker or disloyal friend, or full of envy for someone who has what seem to be undeserved blessings. Or of a person who suffers from a debilitating fear: fear of others or loneliness or the night or poverty or illness or death.

These feelings—hatred, envy, and fear—make no one happy, especially the one who suffers from them. But we do not want to give them up. It would be like giving up the possibility of meaning in life. Somehow these demons manage to persuade us that they embody a truth we cannot do without. I had a colleague once who was addicted to smoking. He told me that whenever he thought of what the day might bring, he thought of every event in terms of the cigarette he would have with it or after it. It was the cigarette that gave his experiences meaning.

In Mark, Jesus is healing people, lots of people, by driving out the demons that inhabit them. He is freeing them from their afflictions, whether these are the tortures of disease or tortures of the mind. As we read, we can feel the hope or dream that he might heal us too, might make us whole and free as we have never been.

What would this wholeness and freedom be like? One way to think of it is to say that, if we were healed, it would be as though we had been perfectly healthy, perfectly loved, perfectly understood, ever since we were born; cared for by perfect parents—like Mary and Joseph!—and never infected with the evil spirits that plague us now.

It is not that we would be rich and powerful and famous. We would not be movie stars or generals or great musicians; we would probably not look at all like successes in the eyes of our culture. But we would be able to trust, and be trusted; able to give love and receive love; and able to do these things naturally and easily, without internal conflict. We would be able to act out of this trust and love, in small ways and great, without embarrassment and without fear. We would be free of the unclean spirits that twist within us, free of shame and guilt. We would be what we were made to be. We would be able to love God and our neighbor.

We might even be able to overcome death itself: perhaps not in the sense that we would live somewhere else when this life is over (though that may happen), but in the more immediate sense that we would be able to see death, to contemplate it, without fear and distress. Death would have no dominion over us. Such is the dream of Christian fulfillment.

It is this kind of amazing, barely imaginable blessing that the scribes, experts in propaganda as they are, characterize as demonic or satanic. Jesus is offering the people he heals supreme love, divine forgiveness, holy encouragement; the scribes call this supreme evil. No wonder Jesus is so angry.

How angry is he? Listen: *"Truly I tell you, people will be forgiven for their sins and whatever blasphemies they utter; but whoever blasphemes against the Holy Spirit can never have forgiveness, but is guilty of an eternal sin."*

Blasphemy is a form of speech, calling something foul or unholy or evil. To call the work of the Holy Spirit the work of the devil, as the scribes are doing, is to commit the ultimate blasphemy. This is the unforgiveable sin: to be in the presence of the Holy and call it the satanic.

Why is this sin unforgiveable? All other sins, all other blasphemies, can be forgiven. Jesus himself stands for forgiveness, even for those who kill him. If killing the Son of God can be forgiven, why cannot the sin against the Holy Spirit be forgiven? After all, this sin consists only in speech, not harmful conduct. Why should it be regarded as so serious?

I do not think Jesus saying that if you have ever sinned against the Holy Spirit you can never be forgiven. Rather, the idea is that the deeply cynical stance the scribes are taking, their denial of the reality of what is good, prevents them from seeing what Jesus is doing, from hearing what Jesus is saying, and in this way prevents them from receiving what he is offering, the healing of their souls by the expulsion of their unclean spirits.

Jesus is saying, I can help the person who is in need and knows it, but I cannot help the person who regards me as the evil one. He or she is blocking everything I say or do. So to blaspheme the Holy Spirit is a terrible thing to do, not terrible for the Holy Spirit but for the one who does it.

What happens when we try to connect this reading to our own lives?

There are two big problems. One is the fact that Jesus will not heal us as he seems to have healed the people in the Gospel. We are not to be blessed in the way I described earlier. That is just not going to happen. We must face the fact that we live in a fallen world. As someone once said, the life and death and resurrection of Jesus in one sense changed everything in the world, but in another sense changed nothing, for we still live with the same evils that he faced.

That is true, but Jesus has given us an image of wholeness and health and love, over the horizon as it were, out of which we can live, towards which we can point. We would never have had that image without him. He has given himself to us in another way as well, not only as an example but as a companion. As we face the evils of the world he is with us. As we suffer he is with us.

The second problem is that we, like the scribes, will sometimes not see—will deny or misname—the presence and activity of God, in ourselves, in other people, and in the world. We are incomplete, weak, confused, broken creatures, afflicted with demons that twist and distort us. I think we are bound sometimes to close our eyes to God, to misname God.

In fact I think we do this all the time, every day, for God suffuses the world around us. God is present in what others say and do, in moments of kindness or truth or gentleness, in gestures of understanding, in periods of suffering, to all of which we are at least sometimes blind. God is present within us as well, as the Spirit of life and love. And in all these places we are often blind to God's presence and life. How are we to live and live well on conditions such as these?

I have no ready answer. There is no formula for success. It is our responsibility as living souls to look for, to recognize, and to respond to God at work in the world, even though we know that we will often fail.

We cannot hope to face this dilemma alone. But we do not have to do that. We have each other, in this church and other churches too; we have Jesus, in the gospel, in the Eucharist, and in our lives; and we have the Holy Spirit, at work within us. The task of life is learning to attune ourselves to these sources of blessing and to live in their light.

Most of all, we know that the Spirit of love at the center of the universe loves us, as a parent loves a child. We know that the Spirit will forgive us, if we only ask for forgiveness. We know that the only force that can separate us from that love, that forgiveness, is our own rejection of it.

Let us go forth in peace, rejoicing in the power of the Spirit.

AMEN

Questions

1. We all have experiences of being physically healed. Can you pick one such experience, and reflect on it, and ask yourself what was happening? Was it simply a matter of an antibiotic killing a germ, or was there a more mysterious process at work? What can you say about that process?

Have you ever had the experience of being healed spiritually or emotionally? How did that work?

2. Have you had the experience of healing others, of being a healer? Was this a matter simply of technique or knowledge, or was there a more mysterious process at work? What can you say about it?

3. Were there times in your life when you can now see that you, like the scribes, were blind or deaf to the presence of God before you? Times when you can see that you were aware of God's presence? Can you find a way to build on experiences of both kinds to increase your capacity to be open to God's presence?

4. Can you find moments in your life when you rejected the Holy, and called it the work of the devil? What do you think and feel about those moments now? What can you hope to do about them?

23

"Who Then Is This?"

As you read this passage from Mark about Jesus and his disciples in the storm on the Sea of Galilee, put yourself in the position of the disciples as fully as you can. Who is this Jesus for you? Who are you to him? You can ask the same two questions from your present position in life. Who is this Jesus for you? Who are you to him?

The Gospel of Mark 4:35–41

On that day, when evening had come, he said to them, "Let us go across to the other side." And leaving the crowd behind, they took him with them in the boat, just as he was. Other boats were with him.

A great windstorm arose, and the waves beat into the boat, so that the boat was already being swamped. But he was in the stern, asleep on the cushion; and they woke him up and said to him, "Teacher, do you not care that we are perishing?"

He woke up and rebuked the wind, and said to the sea, "Peace! Be still!" Then the wind ceased, and there was a dead calm.

He said to them, "Why are you afraid? Have you still no faith?" And they were filled with great awe and said to one another, "Who then is this, that even the wind and the sea obey him?"

The Church of the Mediator, June 24, 2012

May the words of my mouth and the meditations of my heart be always acceptable in thy sight, O Lord, my strength and my redeemer.

Today's gospel story looks like a simple one, and in a sense it is. A storm falls upon the boat carrying Jesus and his disciples across the Sea of Galilee; the disciples become afraid they will sink; they wake Jesus, who has been asleep in the stern; Jesus calms the sea and then asks, "*Why are you afraid? Have you still no faith?*" The disciples then ask each other, "Who then is this, that even the wind and the sea obey him?"

At a literal level, this is a display of divine power by Jesus. He has been driving demons out of ill and afflicted people; now he exerts a similar power over another dangerous thing, the storm at sea.

But that does not tell us much about what the story means, either to the disciples or to us. It may not even be clear to the disciples that Jesus' power is divine, rather than demonic. Their question—"Who then is this, that even the wind and the sea obey him?"—seems to carry a hint of anxiety on this point.

What Jesus says to the disciples is also puzzling. He seems to imply that if the disciples had faith they would not have awakened him. They would have been unafraid and trusting even when in danger. So is Jesus saying something like this, to them and to us: "If you believe and trust in me, everything will be all right"?

But when we look at our own experience we know that everything will not be all right. In the story Jesus chastises the disciples for waking him, but what were they supposed to have done? If they had not waked him would they all have drowned, including Jesus? We do not know, but it is hard to believe that everything would have been all right.

If we look at the life of Jesus himself, the idea that everything will be all right seems even more impossible. We know he is going to be seized, tried in a kangaroo court, abused and humiliated, then tortured to death on the cross. That does not seem to be all right, not at all. To imagine Jesus telling the disciples and us that if only we have faith everything will be all right just seems wrong.

What then are we to make of this passage? We might begin with the question the disciples ask: "Who then is this?" It is our question too.

In one sense of course the disciples know who Jesus is. They have lived with him—seen the healings, watched the crowds, witnessed the miracles. They have been physically with him, as we are with each other in this room. They know the expressions of his face, the tones of his voice, his capacity for gentleness and ferocity, his sense of certainty and doubt. They know what he does and how he talks.

But they still do not fully know him. In Mark's Gospel Jesus repeatedly emphasizes this fact. Again and again, the disciples do not understand, do not believe, do not get who Jesus is and what he is doing. *"Why are you afraid? Have you still no faith?"*

If we look through the whole of Mark's Gospel for a deeper understanding of Jesus, we will find that Mark does not make many explicit statements about who Jesus is. He says almost nothing by way of explicit theology: nothing about the Trinity, for example, or Jesus' birth or origins, and no explanation of where he fits in the history of Judaism. Rather, the sense we get from Mark is that Jesus is a kind of mysterious flame passing through the world transforming all he touches. His preaching is extremely simple, consisting of little more than "The kingdom of God has come near; repent and believe in the Good News." He is urgent and mysterious. He does not explain things.

Likewise, his teaching does not take the form of rules of conduct or other general propositions, like the Sermon on the Mount. Rather, when he teaches he does so mostly in parables, which are by their nature puzzling and mysterious.

All this makes us ask, with the disciples, all the more energetically, "Who then is this?" Mark does not seem to offer any very clear or satisfactory answer.

Why not? Think of Mark's situation. The most extraordinary and amazing person in the history of the world had lived and died in Palestine, and risen from the dead. Perhaps Mark knew him personally; surely he knew people who did. When it became apparent that Jesus was not going to return soon, Mark had the idea—original with him—of writing a text that would represent Jesus to the world in a way that could be the foundation for the Christian community.

But how is Mark going to represent Jesus, the flaming mystery of divine power?

Imagine that today you tried to explain who Jesus is to people who have no idea. How could you possibly do it? Any effort we made would soon collapse either into dead clichés, empty phrases, and stick figure stories or into theological assertions that did not illuminate and explanations that did not explain. We would feel helpless. It would be impossible.

I think Mark has an interesting and surprising solution to this problem. His idea is not to *describe* Jesus, not to *tell us* "who he is" at all—which he cannot do—but something very different. He is trying to give us an idea of *what it was like to know him*. To do this, he tries to replicate in his text the experience of those who actually knew him.

When we read this passage we feel just what the disciples seem to feel: puzzled, frustrated, on the edge of something amazing and wonderful that we cannot comprehend but can half sense, confronted with a truth we cannot translate into other terms. We feel that Jesus is wonderful, but we cannot make sense of him.

This is exactly what Mark thinks the experience of the disciples was like. He is not telling us who Jesus is; he is not explaining him. He is showing us, in the mysterious and frustrating experience he offers, what it is like to be with him. Like Jesus, Mark refuses to give us the explanations that we want, but that won't work.

The truth is that Jesus is beyond us, just as he is beyond Mark. He is not just the Holy One, not just a martyr; he is not reducible to any theory or concept or name. He is a presence, an active reality, representing a wholly new kind of life, and calling us to it—a life we cannot understand but can only dimly begin to feel or see.

As Mark represents him, Jesus is simultaneously revealed to his disciples and hidden from them; likewise he is simultaneously revealed to us, as readers, and hidden from us.

Think of his parables: they work the way Jesus does, not at an intellectual level, but much more immediately, both revealing and hiding the truth. It is true that we are told that Jesus sometimes explains the meaning of the parables to his disciples, but if you look at the only explanation we have, the one about the parable of the sower, you will see that compared to the parable itself it is rather mechanical and dull. What Jesus means, who Jesus is, cannot be reduced to an explanation, even for his disciples.

Now there is one way, and an important one, in which Mark does tell us something central about Jesus' identity. At Jesus' baptism, the voice from heaven says, "This is my Son, the Beloved." After his death, the centurion says, "Truly, this man was God's son." These two statements frame the whole gospel. They sum up who Jesus is, in just the way Mark elsewhere avoids. They are important.

But they do not tell us what it *means* to say that Jesus is the Son of God. That phrase, like Jesus himself, simultaneously reveals a divine truth and obscures it.

When we bring this passage, this gospel, to our own lives and time, I think we can see that it is true to what we know and who we are.

We are invited by Jesus and his church not to inhabit a world of theological declarations, not to desire a set of sentences about who Jesus is, not to seek understanding of an intellectual sort, but to inhabit our own experience of his mystery and force, of his love and his grief—an experience that is so real and vital that it can be, that it should be, the center of our whole lives. It is an experience that remains in important ways beyond us, certainly beyond our minds, but to which our faith can always connect us.

So we are not to ask "what Jesus means" by this statement he makes or that question he asks, as though what he said could be translated into other terms—as though our minds could grasp his truth. We are to accept that we do not and cannot know his truth that way, but we are also to recognize that, if we allow him to do so, Jesus will speak to the center of our souls in ways we can deeply understand.

To live with joy and hope and love in the place that Jesus defines for us is to live in faith. To live in faith does not mean the end of suffering or grief or loss; but if we could do it I think it would mean the end of fear—fear of storms, fear of death. It would also mean that, at the very deepest level of the life of the soul, everything would be all right after all, for we would be living the lives for which we are made.

AMEN

Questions

1. Look at the story as if you were one of the disciples. The storm comes, you are afraid, and you find yourself asking, "Teacher, do you not care that we are perishing?" Who is the Jesus to whom you ask that question? Where does this question come from, from what place within you?

2. Later you ask, "Who then is this, that even the wind and sea obey him?" Who is Jesus to you here? Where does this question come from, from what place within you? What do you mean by it?

What if anything have you learned between the two sentences?

3. Jesus asks, "*Why are you afraid? Have you still no faith?*" How do you respond to this question within yourself? What is the faith that Jesus wishes you had?

4. We have been asking who Jesus is to us. There is another side to the question: who are we to Jesus? Here take some time, shut your eyes, and try to imagine who it is that Jesus sees when he looks at you.

5. If you were to make a prayer based on your experience of this reading, what would it be?

24

"Whoever Believes Has Eternal Life"

In the following passage from John's Gospel, Jesus says, "*Whoever believes has eternal life.*" There are two large questions here: what does he mean by "belief," and what is the nature of the "eternal life" he promises the believer? As you read the passage, ask yourself how you would respond to these questions.

The Gospel of John 6:45–51

"It is written in the prophets, 'And they shall all be taught by God.' Everyone who has heard and learned from the Father comes to me. Not that anyone has seen the Father except the one who is from God; he has seen the Father.

"Very truly, I tell you, whoever believes has eternal life. I am the bread of life. Your ancestors ate the manna in the wilderness, and they died. This is the bread that comes down from heaven, so that one may eat of it and not die. I am the living bread that came down from heaven.

"Whoever eats of this bread will live forever; and the bread that I will give for the life of the world is my flesh."

The Church of the Mediator, August 12, 2012

May the words of my mouth and the meditations of my heart be always acceptable in thy sight, O Lord, my strength and my redeemer.

The words of Jesus we just heard are part of a speech he gives to certain Jews who have been complaining about his claim to be "the bread that came down from heaven." They see this as a blasphemous claim that what Jesus offers is superior to the manna that came to the people of Israel in the desert. In this speech Jesus boldly makes that claim explicit, saying that the people of Israel ate the manna but still died, while people who eat the bread he brings will live forever.

Today I want to focus attention on something Jesus says not about the bread, but about belief: "*Very truly, I tell you, whoever believes has eternal life.*" For some people this is the core of John's Gospel, maybe the core of the gospel itself.

There are two huge theological themes here, "belief" and "eternal life," both very difficult.

We can start with belief: what does Jesus mean when he says, "*Very truly, I tell you, whoever believes has eternal life*"?

Sometimes people think he is saying that belief alone ensures salvation. But can this be right? Does it really not matter what we do, or who we are, or how we treat other people—whether we are greedy, selfish, lustful, and merciless—so long as we do this thing called "believing"?

And what is this belief of which Jesus is talking? Is it an assertion, or a feeling, or a claim, or an assent to a proposition? Is it enough just to say, "We believe"?

As Mother Paula reminded us last week, the Greek word we translate as "believe" has a basic meaning of "trust," and we know that true trust requires wholehearted commitment. So the belief of which Jesus is speaking is not a superficial assent to the truth of theological propositions—the flick of an internal switch from no to yes, which we can then forget about—but a deep and transforming trust from the center of our being.

That trust commits us to a lifelong interaction with Jesus, as he is present both in the gospels and in our hearts. We know that these interactions will not be easy or comfortable, for Jesus demands of us more than we can do—most plainly when he says that we should love our God with all our hearts and love our neighbors as ourselves, neither which is wholly possible for us.

The point of Jesus' difficult engagements with us is not to make life comfortable or easy, but to help us respond ever more deeply to the presence of God in the world and in ourselves. They lead us towards a life in which we can be transformed from the center out.

So our task is not just to affirm something called "belief" but to live out of a trusting commitment that reorients our souls at the center. That commitment is, I think, part of what Jesus meant by "belief."

If we can believe in this committed way, Jesus says, we shall have "eternal life." But what is the eternal life of which he speaks?

We are tempted to think of it as simply eternal satisfaction of our own desires and fantasies. So we think it means something like life on the other side of the pearly gates, in the clouds, with the harps, where we are given everything we lacked on earth. It is an ideal human existence that goes on forever. I don't think that is right. But I have to confess that after a lot of thought over many years, I don't really have a clear idea of what Jesus means by eternal life. If I try to imagine it my mind collapses.

Consider just one example: our life here, the only life we know, is at its heart a life in time, a life of growth and decay and change. Every minute of our day is a minute in the river of time, sweeping us on. Time is the medium in which thought takes place, in which music can be heard, in which we grow and learn. It is the medium in which we say hello and goodbye, the medium in which we learn to love and in which we express that love. Time is the essence of what we know as life.

How can this kind of life be eternal? Eternal life, as it is usually represented, has no time, no change, no growth or decay, no learning. So what can Jesus mean?

Here is one possibility, not the only one of course, but still a possibility: Jesus is not really talking about life after death at all, about our egos going on forever in some other and better place, but about the nature and quality of the life he is offering us here and now, on earth, a life that is truly alive. The life to which Jesus calls us is participation in the spirit of God:

the spirit that can never die, cannot be killed, can never be exterminated. That is true life, eternal life, and it happens now. Right now. In this room.

What is opposed to this true life, this eternal life? Life without God, a life in which we live selfishly, in which we spend our energies seeking money or power or prestige, or perhaps merely entertainment or empty pleasure—a life in which we try to get what we want, as if that would make us happy. Much of the advertising that dominates our world promotes just such a vision of human felicity: happiness as self-satisfaction.

But I think that for Jesus that kind of life is in fact a kind of death. It is from this death, death in life, that he has come to save us, calling us to share in the eternal life that he offers us now—here, today, tomorrow—as we try to live in the way he teaches.

This eternal life is at heart a life of love: love of others, which means not just feelings of desire or affection but mutual connection, mutual responsiveness, mutual responsibility; and love of God—God in the natural world; God in other people's hearts and minds; and God in ourselves, deep within. Both love of God and love of neighbor call us to give up ourselves for the sake of others. We are to love with our whole hearts.

This kind of love is the fulfillment of our deepest natures. It is true life, eternal life.

So I say. But in what sense is this life *eternal*? We might begin by thinking of our experience in this church. Here people give of themselves to our shared life in a thousand ways, from caring for the altar and the grounds to providing music or reading Scripture, to running French markets and food pantries and tutoring programs, to caring for the building, to managing our finances, to teaching our children. I could go on and on, referring to every single person in this room, who, inspired by the Spirit, helps create this life.

What is the effect of what we do? It is to build this church, this community of the Holy Spirit. This church will outlive all of us. If by chance it should close its doors, its members will go to other churches, and those churches will live on. The life of this church truly is a piece of the life that is eternal, of the God who cannot be killed.

Each of us has other "churches" too: families and friendships and classrooms and medical offices and businesses and other communities in which the Spirit can also live, if we allow it to do so, even if it is never named. Here, too, we can participate in the life that is eternal.

To say that this life is eternal, as I do, is to affirm a faith, a faith that is resisted by much of our experience, a faith that, in the end, the life of the Spirit, the force of goodness and love, will always overcome the forces of hate and evil—the faith that God cannot be killed. There are times when this is hard to believe, but I do believe it. The Source of life is always present, always creating, always healing, always moving us toward the light. This is one of the meanings of the Resurrection.

I believe all this is part of what Jesus meant. But what about the topic I have brushed aside, eternal life after death? Surely Jesus is talking about that as well?

I do think Jesus is talking about life after death: about eternal life not only here and now, but there and then. As I say, I cannot really imagine that life—it is a mystery beyond my mind, perhaps beyond all our minds—but the promise has been made to us, and made by one whom we should trust before all others.

Perhaps we can get a little sense of it by using a familiar image or metaphor. Think of the life of a seed, dark and cold in the workshop closet. It knows nothing but that darkness and coldness until it is planted in moist earth, in the heat of the sun, and then watered and fed. Then it cracks and breaks open—in this sense it dies—and bursts into a kind of life it could not possibly have imagined: it becomes a green shoot rising straight to the sun. Maybe it becomes a flower, brilliant yellow against the green. Or think of a human baby coming into this world, a world unlike anything he or she has known, a baby ready to love and be loved. This baby will grow into a full human being in a way that no one who had not already seen it happen could possibly imagine.

These are facts of our world. Maybe our movement to eternal life will be like that of the baby or the seed: unimaginable ahead of time but when it happens the realest thing of all.

I think it is right for us to have the faith that an eternal life awaits us when we die: a life we cannot imagine, in a world we cannot imagine, but in which we can believe and trust.

AMEN

Questions

1. How would you describe your own fundamental faith or belief? Is this, as I have suggested, really a form of trust?

2. How would you describe your sense of the eternal life that Jesus promises us?

3. What happens when you try to answer these two questions? You will probably find that they are in a real sense impossible. No adequate answer can be given to them. Our language breaks down when we try to respond openly and fairly to them. If so, the question becomes, "What does this impossibility, this breakdown, mean for our own understanding of Scripture, of ourselves, and of our God?" What do you think?

4. If you were to compose a prayer after reading and thinking about this passage, what would it be?

25

"You Are the Messiah"

Who is Jesus? In the passage below Peter identifies him as the Messiah. What do you suppose that term meant to Peter? To Jesus?

Jesus then tells his disciples about his coming death and resurrection. Peter rebukes him. Why does he do that? Jesus responds forcefully, "Get behind me, Satan!" Why does he do that?

The Gospel of Mark 8:27–38

Jesus went on with his disciples to the villages of Caesarea Philippi; and on the way he asked his disciples, "Who do people say that I am?" And they answered him, "John the Baptist; and others, Elijah; and still others, one of the prophets."

He asked them, "But who do you say that I am?" Peter answered him, "You are the Messiah." And he sternly ordered them not to tell anyone about him.

Then he began to teach them that the Son of Man must undergo great suffering, and be rejected by the elders, the chief priests, and the scribes, and be killed, and after three days rise again. He said all this quite openly.

And Peter took him aside and began to rebuke him. But turning and looking at his disciples, he rebuked Peter and said, "Get behind me, Satan! For you are setting your mind not on divine things but on human things."

He called the crowd with his disciples, and said to them, "If any want to become my followers, let them deny themselves and take up their cross and follow me. For those who want to save their life will lose it, and those who lose their life for my sake, and for the sake of the gospel, will save it. For what will it profit them to gain the whole world and forfeit their life? Indeed, what can they give in return for their life? Those who are ashamed of me and of my words in this adulterous and sinful generation, of them the Son of Man will also be ashamed when he comes in the glory of his Father with the holy angels."

The Church of the Mediator, September 16, 2012

May the words of my mouth and the meditations of my heart be always acceptable in thy sight, O Lord, my strength and my redeemer.

In our gospel reading today Jesus asks his disciples, "*Who do you say that I am?*" and Peter answers, "You are the Messiah." Most of us know that this answer is both right and wrong. Jesus is indeed the Messiah, but he is not the Messiah Peter imagines.

In Hebrew *Messiah* literally meant "anointed person," but the only people who fell into that category in the Hebrew Bible were kings, above all David—the king who united the kingdoms of Judah and Israel in a reign marked by military prowess and economic success. It is this kind of Messiah that Peter seems to have in mind. Jesus corrects him, saying that the Son of Man (his own title for himself) must suffer and be rejected by the authorities of Israel and be killed, and then rise again.

That is the kind of Messiah I am, Jesus is saying, not the kind you expect. Peter simply cannot take this, and, being Peter, he begins to rebuke Jesus, whereupon Jesus says his famous words: "*Get behind me, Satan! For you are setting your mind not on divine things but on human things.*"

Peter's mistake, about the kind of Messiah Jesus will prove to be, is important to us because we make mistakes just like it, mistakes, that is, about the right way to pay attention to the relationship between what we are taught in Scripture and our own experience of life.

For when Peter says Jesus is the Messiah, I am pretty sure he is relying on what Scripture predicts, not on what he personally knows of Jesus from his own experience of him. His attention is on what he has been led to expect or hope, not on what is before him. This is what leads him to his mistake. We should not be quick to blame Peter. He is doing what we all do, all the time, for we all try to understand our new experiences by reference to what we already know. We all use the old to interpret the new. We go from the known to the unknown. That is how we learn and grow.

Thus it is that when Peter sees that Jesus is even more astonishing than he and his friends have been able to recognize or express, a person utterly unique with a unique relation to God, he naturally uses a label his Scripture and tradition have given him: "You are the Messiah."

In this statement Peter expresses both great insight and real distortion. Jesus *is* the chosen one of God, that is right; but he has not come to create a regime like David's, a kingly regime of economic and military power. In fact he will do the absolute opposite: he will become an embodiment of weakness, of nonresistance, of sacrifice, of forgiveness, of love. He will not kill, but be killed.

No one could foresee this. Peter cannot really believe it even when Jesus tells him. He certainly cannot register what Jesus means when he says he will rise again.

The personal *experience* that Peter is trying to make sense of is his experience of Jesus himself, which is utterly amazing and utterly puzzling. The cultural *knowledge* that Peter brings to bear on this experience is his knowledge of the Messiah who is predicted in Scripture. So he mislabels Jesus. In fact the reality of Jesus cannot be captured by the knowledge Peter brings to it. Jesus is more amazing, more astonishing, than anything he can find to say.

In this passage we are thus shown a double truth: Scripture and the tradition built upon it were a great help to Peter, for without them he would not have had the idea or word *Messiah*; but this word was also a hindrance to him, for it has meanings that do not fit the new and stunning reality of Jesus.

In this story Peter stands for us, and his problem is our problem too. Like him, we inhabit an inherited Scripture and tradition, which shape our minds and expectations. To take an obvious example, think of the image of God that we often have as children, mainly derived from certain readings in the Old Testament: God as an old man with a beard, in the sky, demanding obedience and threatening punishment. We all know how hard it can be to grow into a more mature understanding of God, and how impossible it is to express that understanding. The truth is that God is beyond our minds, beyond our language.

We are also like Peter in the mysteriousness of our present experience of God. Although we do not live in the company of Jesus as Peter did, we do live in the presence of the living God. I believe that we all have experiences of the Holy, in church and in life, which transcend our powers of understanding and expression.

What kind of experiences do I mean? Nothing could be harder to talk about, for all these experiences are in a real way inexpressible and mysterious, and no doubt we each have our own sense of God's presence (or absence). But it may be worth saying that some of our experiences might be very simple things: a perception of peace and serenity on coming into church in the morning; a feeling of oneness with the universe at the sight of the sun coming through the trees; a sense of perfect beauty watching two of our older grandchildren treating a young cousin with kindness; the awe with which we are filled at the immense variety and beauty of the natural world; the feeling in a prayer group that somehow the presence of the Lord is in this place; or an awareness of the spirit of God alive within our souls, drawing us on towards something new, or drawing us back from something we should not do. Some people of course have much more dramatic experiences, of angels, say, or direct visions of God. But we cannot all have those things.

The question for us, as for Peter, is what is the right relation between these two parts of life, Scripture and experience? Or, to put it in terms of attention, when and how should we direct our attention to Scripture and tradition? When and how should we direct our attention to our own immediate experience of God?

There are two obvious dangers. First, like Peter, we can give too much authority to the Scriptures—to our theological preconceptions, to the past.

We behave this way when we think of the Creed, for example, as a self-contained system of truth, complete in itself and requiring nothing from us except acceptance. "The Holy Spirit proceeds from the Father and the Son," we say, as though saying that alone somehow put us on the right side, with God, even if it means very little in our actual lives.

A side of us really does want to assume that Scripture says it all. This is the Word of God after all. But if we paid attention only to Scripture and lived as if that were the only reality, we would not be fully alive, nor would the Scriptures be fully alive in us. We would be like the law student who masters a system of law in the books and has no idea how to connect it to life. When Peter makes this mistake, Jesus tells him he is thinking of human things, not divine things.

The other mistake we could make, and perhaps a side of us wants to do this too, is to think that our own experience of the Holy is everything, Scripture nothing, that we have nothing to learn, nothing to gain, from our tradition, from its texts and images and practices. Ralph Waldo Emerson once said that if God could reveal himself in Palestine two thousand years ago, he can reveal himself now, to me. This impulse has its own appeal, sometimes a deep appeal, but I think it would ultimately lead us away from God, not towards him.

The truth is that we need the Scriptures, as we need the practices and sacraments and community of the church. We need them even at moments of private and mystical insight. We need them to direct our attention, to teach us what to look for and what to listen to; we need them to give us a language in which we can approach and try to express our experience. This language will of course often be inadequate, sometimes misleading—as the term *Messiah* is for Peter. But we could do virtually nothing without it. We would be on our own, alone. To try to do that would be to deny a holy source of life.

That is all true. But it is also true that we should not let the Scriptures block out the realities of our own lives, blinding us to what is right before us, or within us—as Peter was partly blinded to the reality of Jesus. That, too, would be to deny a holy source of life.

The Christian life requires us to attend both to the Scriptures and to our own experience, living in a mutually corrective interaction between them. God is in the Scriptures, in the tradition, and in the church; God is also within us, within others around us, and in our hearts. We need always strive to open ourselves to this double reality. Just as every human being lives on the razor-thin edge between the past and the future, the Christian lives on the edge between Scripture and experience. Hard as it may be, it is our task to put them together. That is what Jesus is saying to Peter. There is no easy way to do this of course. It is a task for a life, to be addressed anew every day.

A final word. When we begin to attend to this double reality of Scripture and experience we may begin to see more fully that the dichotomy between them can be a false one. In today's gospel, for example, Jesus presents himself as a source of utter newness to his friends, who are right before him, but he is also present to us as we read what he says and does, and he is making us a similar offer. For us Jesus is in Scripture, but he offers us something like the experience of newness that he offers his disciples. This is a newness that even Peter cannot grasp, and we cannot either. Who can make sense of the Crucifixion and Resurrection? Peter cannot, and I think we cannot either—though we can live in their light. Like him, we are brought to face a mystery in the living present.

Jesus is present in this text, offering us a life we cannot comprehend and cannot realize. In this sense Scripture is offering us not a relic of past, but the experience of the living presence of Jesus himself. If we really hear what Jesus says, we will be brought, like Peter, to think as we have never thought, to feel as we have never felt. No language, no set of expectations, can be adequate to this task.

Think of Jesus' sentence, "*Those who want to save their life will lose it, and those who lose their life for my sake, and the sake of the Gospel, will save it.*" When we read that, we cannot just nod and say yes. We cannot place it in a neat theological system. It calls upon us to reimagine our whole lives. Of course we cannot do this fully, but in making the attempt we may find ourselves on the edge of a life of a wholly new kind.

God is present both in the Scriptures and in the world, and in both places as a source of unending life for us.

AMEN

Questions

1. Can you think of experiences of the Holy in your own life that cannot be fully expressed or reduced to language? What would it be like to try to live out of those experiences alone? Could you do it?

2. Can you think of ways in which you, like Peter, want to live out of the language and images of Scripture, and the rituals and traditions of the church, and to use them to shape and define your experience? What would it be like to try to live solely out of Scripture and the tradition built upon it?

3. Can you imagine yourself caught in the space between these two things, Scripture and experience, trying to make your own way? What is it like to try to do that?

4. When you do try, can you say of yourself what the Shaker hymn says, that you are "coming down where you ought to be"?

26

The Rich Young Man

The passage we read today is one of the most uncomfortable in the gospels. In it Jesus tells the rich young man to sell all he has and give the money to the poor. How are we to live with this commandment?

The Gospel of Mark 10:17–31

As he was setting out on a journey, a man ran up and knelt before him, and asked him, "Good Teacher, what must I do to inherit eternal life?"

Jesus said to him, "Why do you call me good? No one is good but God alone. You know the commandments: 'You shall not murder; You shall not commit adultery; You shall not steal; You shall not bear false witness; You shall not defraud; Honor your father and mother.'"

He said to him, "Teacher, I have kept all these since my youth." Jesus, looking at him, loved him and said, "You lack one thing; go, sell what you own, and give the money to the poor, and you will have treasure in heaven; then come, follow me." When he heard this, he was shocked and went away grieving, for he had many possessions.

Then Jesus looked around and said to his disciples, "How hard it will be for those who have wealth to enter the kingdom of God!" And the disciples were perplexed at these words.

But Jesus said to them again, "Children, how hard it is to enter the kingdom of God! It is easier for a camel to go through the eye of a needle than for someone who is rich to enter the kingdom of God."

They were greatly astounded and said to one another, "Then who can be saved?" Jesus looked at them and said, "For mortals it is impossible, but not for God; for God all things are possible."

Peter began to say to him, "Look, we have left everything and followed you." Jesus said, "Truly I tell you, there is no one who has left house or brothers or sisters or mother or father or children or fields, for my sake and for the sake of the good news, who will not receive a hundredfold now in this age—houses, brothers and sisters, mothers and children, and fields, with persecutions—and in the age to come eternal life. But many who are first will be last, and the last will be first."

The Church of the Mediator, October 14, 2012

May the words of my mouth and the meditations of my heart be always acceptable in thy sight, O Lord, my strength and my redeemer.

THE GOSPEL PASSAGE WE heard today is uncomfortable in the extreme. When we hear Jesus tell the rich young man to sell all he owns and give the money to the poor, I think a lot of us squirm in our seats. I know I do. When we are told that it is easier for a camel to go through the eye of a needle than for a rich person to enter the kingdom of God, we squirm again.

We are not the only ones. People have spent a lot of energy and talent trying to wriggle out of what seems to be the plain meaning of these sayings of Jesus. About the rich young man, I have been told, for example:

1. When the man is told to sell *what he owns*, that means he should sell his personal property—jewelry maybe, furniture and urns, rich clothing, stuff like that—but certainly not the real estate on which his income depends, not his farms and houses.

2. When he is told to *give the money* to the poor, what that really means is that he should give the poor alms, perhaps in the traditional amount of 10 percent.

About the rich man, the camel, and the eye of a needle I have been told:

3. The phrase "eye of the needle" *has nothing to do with the needle you use in sewing.* It is a reference to a small gate in the walls of Jerusalem, which was kept open after the others were closed. This gate was so narrow and low that a camel could not get through it without the removal of its saddlebags. This sounds good, but so far as I can tell, there is no truth in it.

4. *The word* camel *is a mistranslation* arising from a copyist's error. The proper Greek word meant "hawser" or "cable." But there is no evidence that there was such a copyist's error, so far as I know, and, in any event, it is not much better to speak of a hawser than a camel trying to get through the eye of a needle.

5. Finally, I have been told by a well-known clergyman that we should completely disregard both passages because when Jesus said these things he did not know what we know, which is that under a capitalist system like ours the concentration of wealth in the hands of a few is a good thing for everyone. To give money to the poor is pure sentimentality. If Jesus were alive today he would never say such things.

I have been making fun of these specious rationalizations (and there are more), but we need to recognize that they are made in distress by people like us—people like the rich young man in the story—who find Jesus' command impossible to obey and cannot endure it. What, then, are we to do with these disturbing passages? We all seem to want to rip them apart.

Let's return to the text itself. The story begins when Jesus is about to set forth on a journey. A young man runs up to him and kneels before him, asking, "Good Teacher, what must I do to inherit eternal life?"

We see something already about the personality of the young man. He runs; he kneels; he is eager and intense. Maybe he is also a little conflicted, and that is why he waited to approach Jesus until he was on the brink of departure.

Jesus tells him that he must obey the traditional commandments, to which the young man answers, "I have kept all these since my youth."

Something wonderful happens at this moment: we are told that Jesus "loved him." What does this mean? Why does Jesus love him especially, and especially now? Is it his intensity, his eagerness, his openness? His trust in Jesus? His sense that although he obeys the commandments that is somehow not enough?

Jesus' response may seem hard on him: "*You lack one thing; go, sell what you own, and give the money to the poor, and you will have treasure in heaven; then come, follow me.*" But I think that Jesus gives the young man this extra commandment because he loves him so much. This command is not meant as a burden, but as a gift. Jesus gives it to him because he knows he needs more than the commandments. No wonder Jesus loves him. He is a rare person indeed.

Then Jesus makes him another gift, inviting him to come with him on the journey to Jerusalem he is about to start. He calls him to become a disciple.

But the young man simply cannot do what Jesus asks, and goes away grieving deeply. You can see what he might be thinking: "I can keep the commandments: no murder, no theft, no lying, and so forth. But he is asking me to give away all my property, and I just cannot do that."

Jesus then says to his disciples, "*How hard it will be for those who have wealth to enter the kingdom of God!*"—adding that it is easier for a camel to go through the eye of a needle than for a rich person to enter the kingdom of God.

I think that in saying this Jesus is still thinking about the young man. He is lamenting the fact that this man could not give up everything to follow him. Jesus is not being condemnatory here, but loving and sympathetic. He is feeling sorry for the rich.

What is it about wealth that Jesus has in mind? I think it may be something that is at once simple and complex: the power that wealth has over the minds and feelings of those who have it. The young man could not leave his wealth and follow Jesus, as the disciples who were fishermen left their work, but was kept away from him by a tie he could not cut. He could not free himself from his pattern of life.

In what he says to the disciples Jesus is not attacking the injustices of wealth, or the evil that rich people do, but something very different: he is expressing his sympathetic awareness that wealth can cripple and distort the soul of one who possesses it.

The major expression of the unhappy state of the young man's soul is of course his act of turning way from Jesus. But a piece of it was present at the very beginning, in the question he asked: "Good Teacher, what must I do to inherit eternal life?" That may seem an innocuous question, but if you think about what he takes for granted when he asks it, it becomes more troubling. What the young man is assuming is that there is, or ought to be, something he can do that will bring him eternal life.

I think we hear in this question, that is, the voice of the person with privilege, the person whose stance towards life is to ask what he wants and how he can get it, working on the premise that of course he can get it if he can only figure out how. A person with privilege of this kind is often completely blind to the assumptions of entitlement he is making, assumptions that some others would not dream of making.

For wealth does not mean only that one can buy things others cannot buy; it helps create a mode of life, a set of assumptions, an unrecognized sense of entitlement and privilege, which are the very things the young man cannot give up. Compare with the young man's question, for example, the prayer of the publican in the gospel story about the Pharisee and the publican: "Lord, have mercy on me, a sinner." That, not the Pharisee's prayer of self-satisfaction, is the prayer of life. "How do I get . . .?" is not a prayer of life.

What the story shows is that even for a good person (and the young man is very good) wealth is bad, bad for him that is. It ties him to something he cannot escape. It keeps him from saying yes to Jesus' call. Even though Jesus is sympathetic, what he says is still devastating. He is saying that the rich have chosen or made a life that bars them from accepting the love of Jesus, and not only in heaven but in the kingdom now, on earth. That is a terrible thing to hear.

So now we get to the question that has been on all of your minds: just how rich do we have to be to suffer from the disabilities of the young man in the story?

I cannot answer this for sure, but it is plain that we don't have to be loaded. Look at the disciples, none of whom was by any normal measure wealthy, but who, when they heard the story, applied it to themselves, and said to Jesus, "Then who can be saved?" That is in fact the central question of this whole passage, and Jesus answers it this way: "*For mortals it is impossible.*" That is his real answer to the issue raised by the young man's question, "What must I do to inherit eternal life?" It is impossible.

What Jesus is saying, then, to his disciples and to us, is something like this: "There is nothing you can do to inherit eternal life. Your salvation is not among those things that you can control through your wealth, your intelligence, your social competence, your connections with the powerful, or anything else. There is nothing you can do to inherit eternal life."

That does not mean we cannot *have* eternal life. For God all things are possible, even this: to give us salvation freely, defective and weak though we are, as an act of grace and love. It is ours if only we will accept it and not turn away. But the kind of acceptance called for here is the wholehearted acceptance of a new life, closing the door on the old one. It is turning from death to life. This is what the young man cannot do.

It is also what none of us can wholly do. We are very much like this rich young man, for we are tied by something—whether money or pride or selfishness or anger or whatever else consumes us—in such a way that we cannot turn our backs on the old and give ourselves wholly to the new. When Jesus says, "Sell all, give all," we cannot do it. We do not sell all, and we do not give all: not all our property, not all our selves.

So how are we to respond to this difficult passage? We cannot evade it. But I think we can learn from the disciples how to face it. Like them we can acknowledge our inadequacy, our presumptions of entitlement, the other things to which we are tied, and we can ask with our whole hearts, "Then who can be saved?" At the same time we can try to accept the fact, and recognize it in our souls, that salvation is not something we can attain by our own efforts, but is a gift of God.

"Lord, have mercy on me, a sinner."

AMEN

Questions

1. Jesus sees that the young man before him is capable of living the deep and true life he wants in his disciples. But he also sees that he is tied or hampered by his dependence on something else, in this case his wealth, and perhaps the social status it gives him.

   I think the gospel is asking each of us to ask ourselves: on what am I dependent that ties and hampers me, that keeps me from responding to the call Jesus is making? It might be money or prestige or a sense of connection with power or a feeling that we matter in the world. Or it might be another kind of dependence altogether, an addiction, say, to the use of narcotic substances or to a self-defeating pattern of behavior in one's social relations, or it might be an ideology or theory or some other kind of daydreaming that we use as a substitute for reality. What happens when you ask this question of yourself?

2. Is there something especially alluring and seductive and potentially evil about money and what it means? What are the dangers of money for you? How well do you protect yourself from them?

3. What about eternal life? What do you think that phrase means? Is it really true that you can do nothing to attain it, as Jesus seems to say? If so, what does that fact mean for you?

27

Christ the King

In this passage Pilate tries to get Jesus to admit that he claims to be a king. If he succeeds in this, Jesus' punishment for treason will be justified. In response, Jesus first fences verbally with Pilate, with considerable skill, then seems to change the subject entirely: "*For this I was born, and for this I came into the world, to testify to the truth.*" As you read, ask yourself, what is the relation between this statement and the talk about kingship?

Where are you in this story?

The Gospel of John 18:33–37

Then Pilate entered the headquarters again, summoned Jesus, and asked him, "Are you the King of the Jews?"

Jesus answered, "Do you ask this on your own, or did others tell you about me?"

Pilate replied, "I am not a Jew, am I? Your own nation and the chief priests have handed you over to me. What have you done?" Jesus answered, "My kingdom is not from this world. If my kingdom were from this world, my followers would be fighting to keep me from being handed over to the Jews. But as it is, my kingdom is not from here."

Pilate asked him, "So you are a king?"

Jesus answered, "You say that I am a king. For this I was born, and for this I came into the world, to testify to the truth. Everyone who belongs to the truth listens to my voice."

The Church of the Incarnation, November 25, 2012

May the words of my mouth and the meditations of my heart be always acceptable in thy sight, O Lord, my strength and my redeemer.

Today is what we call Christ the King Sunday, a day that is celebrated in many branches of the Christian church. This custom is not an ancient one, but the image of Christ as a King does go all the way back at least to the Book of Revelation.

To me it seems odd to think of Jesus as a king or ruler or magnate of any kind, given what we know about him. So this is the problem I will be talking about today: how, if at all, is Christ a king?

The topic of kingship comes up in today's Gospel when Pilate demands of Jesus, "Are you the King of the Jews?" Jesus answers with another question: "*Do you ask this on your own, or did others tell you about me?*" Pilate says he is acting on the wishes of others: "Your own nation and the chief priests have handed you over to me. What have you done?"

Jesus again does not answer, but returns to the topic of kingship in a different way: "*My kingdom is not from this world.*" If it were, he says, "*my followers would be fighting to keep me from being handed over.*" Pilate seizes his opportunity, and asks, "So you are a king?" Jesus responds, "*You say that I am king,*" that is, it is you who is making that claim, not me. Jesus then turns completely away from this verbal dance and says, "*For this I was born, and for this I came into the world, to testify to the truth. Everyone who belongs to the truth listens to my voice.*"

Jesus denies he is a king of one kind, a king of this world, but at the same time he claims, paradoxically, that he is king of another kind, "*not from this world.*" What sense can we make of this passage?

To start with, when we look at the present condition of the world, it is pretty obvious that Jesus is not a universal king, in total control of everything. There is far too much human suffering and evil for this to be the case. Think of it: constant wars, human trafficking, suffering children, billions of desperately hungry people, the destruction of the living organism we call the earth. I cannot believe that this is the world Jesus would make if he were its universal king.

What is more, if we look at Jesus' life, we can see that he was in most respects the opposite of a king. Kingship is a form of power, perhaps the ultimate form. Jesus divested himself of power throughout his life in every way.

He was tempted by the devil to assume power over the world, and he rejected it. Likewise he told his friends, and us, that we should divest ourselves of power too: if a man strike you on the cheek, offer him the other; if he demand your cloak, give him your tunic also. To the rich young man, whose riches were so important to him, he said, sell what you own and give the money to the poor. He told us all to practice forgiveness, which is the deliberate renunciation of an important kind of power, the power of blaming and resentment.

I think Jesus is showing us how to live on purpose without power. He is trying to free us from the anxiety and fear that makes us think that power is necessary to our happiness or safety—the fear that if we do not control others they will control us and if we lose power we will have nothing.

He is also trying to protect us from what happens to those who do have power. The person in power, perhaps unwittingly, reduces other human beings to mere objects of control. He or she tends not to treat them as people entitled to life and autonomy and respect, but as instruments. In doing this to us, power destroys our capacity to love.

Jesus came to free us from our love of power so that we might be free to love one another, not only in the church but in the world.

But how can we live without power? The very thought challenges our basic assumptions about our lives, in which we spend so much of our energy trying to acquire and defend power. I think Jesus would say that we do not need power because we have him, and each other: each other in the church, each other in the family, each other even among strangers on the highway. In place of power, Jesus gives us love: love, and the trust in life itself that love requires.

So Jesus rejects kingship, rejects power. But there is a paradox here, for, as he repeatedly shows us, in weakness there can be an astonishing strength, a strength that can change us and our world. We can see this in our own history, in the civil rights movement, when people of peace and gentleness stood up to power bravely. The power they resisted was not metaphorical but real, often raw and brutal, in the form of sheriffs and nightsticks and dogs and prison. Some people were beaten or brutalized; some were even killed. But they did not fight back. And when their brothers and sisters kept going they created a moral force that could not be resisted.

Like Jesus in this passage, their strength came from the fact that they were testifying to the truth: the truth of their own humanity; the truth of the justice they were denied; the truth that they, and we, and all people, including their abusers, are God's children.

There are more common examples of strength in weakness. When our grandson Oliver was born a couple of years ago I could see that this tiny person—incapable of speech, unable to crawl or sit up, completely dependent—was in his utter weakness immensely strong. He transformed, from the inside out, the lives of his parents, his grandparents, and his uncles and aunts. He still is transforming us, week by week. Without his exactly knowing it, he has been teaching us again and in new ways about the reality and nature of love, about its truth and strength.

Every baby born into the world is like Oliver, ready to love and be loved, calling on us to respond to him or her, teaching us the truth of love that we so often hide in our hearts.

This is strength in weakness. It has its origins in truth and love. It is the presence of the Spirit in the world. In the end there is no greater strength than this.

The greatest example of strength in weakness, the one that validates all the others, is Jesus himself.

In being killed on the Cross, Jesus renounced power in an ultimate way, but from this renunciation came his Resurrection, by which he was present after his death with his friends, two thousand years ago, and by which he is present today: in the gospel passages that live in our minds and hearts; in the Eucharist we celebrate every week; and in the heart of each of us, and among us all, when we gather in his name. This is strength beyond all strength. It cannot be extinguished, no matter how much we or others may try to do so. It lives forever.

So what kind of king is Jesus? Not a king of power, not at all, but a king of love, of truth, of apparent weakness and real strength.

Now how about us? How are we to bring this story to our own lives?

The big problem is that all of us, in our own ways—some more, some less—want to be king or queen. We want to have power, maybe not over the whole world, but over our own environment, our own fate, over what we do and what other people allow us to do, over what we keep and what we spend, over who we know and who we don't, over what we buy and what we sell.

In some ways we do want to run the world, or at least I do. During election season, for example, I am an obsessive tornado, demanding that my candidate win, and afterwards I am almost as busy demanding that he or she do just what I would want. I turn myself into a deeply frustrated imaginary king.

A second problem is this: what makes weakness strength, as Jesus says, is the fact that one is testifying to the truth in love. Are we testifying to the truth? How can we know? This is not something we can be confident about, to put it mildly. In fact we spend lots of time and energy testifying to falseness, and doing so not in love but in anger or hate.

How can we learn to renounce our desire for power, learn to testify to the truth in love, and learn to practice the impossible art of forgiveness?

There is of course no easy answer. It is true, though painful, that if we undergo deep disappointment and frustration this may help us resist the diseases of our own hearts: if we lose our money or become ill or face the humiliations of divorce or unemployment, if we lose, in short, our fantasies of power and control. Affliction can be an act of grace. Of course sometimes it is not that, not at all, but it can be.

Other things can help us too, and thank God for them: the love of a friend or a spouse; the discovery of a piece of the Spirit within us; hearing a call we cannot resist, to stand up to evil; recognizing that in the gospel Jesus is actually speaking to us, to each of us, calling us from death into life, from falseness into truth.

For God is with us, and within us, always calling us, not with the idea that we can lead a perfect life in perfect attunement with the Holy One, but that we can move into life of a new kind, a life in which we struggle to discover and testify to the truth, in which we struggle to give and receive love, in which we struggle to forgive what seems unforgiveable.

AMEN

Questions

1. Are there ways in which you have power in the world, over other people or over resources? What do you feel about this fact, and what can you do about it?

2. Have you ever found yourself weak and vulnerable? What did you feel about that fact and what did you do about it?

3. Have you ever renounced power, or made yourself deliberately weak and vulnerable? Is this what Jesus is calling us to do?

4. Have you ever had the experience of weakness itself paradoxically becoming a source of strength, in yourself or others? Where did the strength come from? Was it because someone was testifying to the truth?

5. If you were to compose a prayer in response to reading this gospel passage, what would it be?

28

Repent or Perish

In the reading from Luke that follows below Jesus tells his listeners to "repent." What does that word mean to you? Do you ever use it of yourself? Can you imagine doing so? If you do not repent, Jesus says, you will perish. What can he mean by "perish"?

The Gospel of Luke 13:1–9

At that very time there were some present who told him about the Galileans whose blood Pilate had mingled with their sacrifices. He asked them, "Do you think that because these Galileans suffered in this way they were worse sinners than all other Galileans? No, I tell you; but unless you repent, you will all perish as they did. Or those eighteen who were killed when the tower of Siloam fell on them—do you think that they were worse offenders than all the others living in Jerusalem? No, I tell you; but unless you repent, you will all perish just as they did."

Then he told this parable: "A man had a fig tree planted in his vineyard; and he came looking for fruit on it and found none. So he said to the gardener, 'See here! For three years I have come looking for fruit on this fig tree, and still I find none. Cut it down! Why should it be wasting the soil?' He replied, 'Sir, let it alone for one more year, until I dig around it and put manure on it. If it bears fruit next year, well and good; but if not, you can cut it down.'"

The Church of the Incarnation, March 3, 2013

May the words of my mouth and the meditations of my heart be always acceptable in thy sight, O Lord, my strength and my redeemer.

There are two parts to today's gospel: the people telling Jesus about Pilate's murder of the Galileans while they were sacrificing, and the parable of the fig tree. I will be focusing mainly on the first part.

Why do you suppose the people tell Jesus about the Galileans? What are they doing when they do that? I think they are really asking a question: how should we respond in our minds and feelings when we hear that someone else has suffered a catastrophe? This is a real question for us too: what should we think and say when another person runs into disaster?

The people seem to think that the Galileans must in some way have deserved their deaths, while they themselves are righteous and therefore safe from calamity. In this way they are distancing themselves from disaster.

This is a common human response. We all do it. When I lived near the University of Chicago, I would frequently hear stories about muggings. The speaker was always sympathetic, but sooner or later he would distance himself from the victim: "He was under the El tracks at 11:00 at night, and I would never do that." Likewise, when we hear of an auto accident we say to ourselves, "He was old or young, or the road was so icy I would never have gone out." Or we hear of a heart attack, and we reassure ourselves with the low-fat diet we do not keep. We are safe.

There is a word for this. It is *denial*. And this is denial of an especially toxic kind, for it denies our connection to other people. It denies our common vulnerability in an uncertain world. It denies our common identity.

It is this position that Jesus attacks, saying in effect, "Don't think that the Galileans are worse than you. Don't pretend that you are not vulnerable to this kind of random disaster, for you are. Don't try to separate yourself from the suffering of other people in this way." This all makes good sense.

Then he adds, "*Unless you repent, you will all perish just as they did.*" What can he mean by these words? They sound harsh and punitive. Is that how Jesus is really talking? Or can we hear what he says as loving, as coming from the Jesus we know?

One way into this problem is to ask what he means by his two key terms, *repent* and *perish*.

To start with repentance, this is a hard subject for us to talk about. "Repentance" can easily seem to us to be part of an outmoded theology in which a punitive God seeks out those who disobey his commands and punishes them unless they "repent." And repenting can sound like crawling on your belly before a demanding deity.

But the first person in the Christian tradition to say "Repent, the kingdom is near" was John the Baptist, and the second was Jesus himself. So we should take this word and what it means with the utmost seriousness.

Our task is to find a way to hear what Jesus is actually saying when he speaks of repentance, not what we imagine some theological bogeyman to be saying.

Let me begin this way. In our prayer book there is a penitential service called The Great Litany, of which I want to read one short bit: "From all blindness of heart; from pride, vainglory, and hypocrisy; from envy, hatred, and malice; and from all want of charity, *Good Lord, deliver us.*"

I love this. The reason I love it is that it reminds me of truths about myself that I deeply want to deny. I want to deny that my heart is often blind, though it is; I want to deny that I suffer from pride, vainglory, and hypocrisy, though I do; and I want to deny that envy, hatred, and malice have a place in my heart and soul, and that I suffer from a want of charity, though all these things are also true. True of me and true of you and true of all of us. The prayer asks us to face these truths, to feel the remorse and sorrow this facing entails.

This is the first stage of repentance. The second is to ask for forgiveness, and to do so in confidence that it will be granted. The third is to accept joyfully the forgiveness we are offered. To enact this complex gesture is to move in the direction of freedom and wholeness. At the end of it we may discover not only that we are forgiven, but that we can forgive. But none of it is easy.

The key thing is to see that our repentance is for our benefit, not God's. It is for our benefit, not because it removes some black marks against us in the book of heaven, but because it makes possible for us a deeper, truer, and more meaningful life.

Repentance is a regeneration and a blessing. For Jesus to ask us to repent is a way of loving us.

Now for the second problem: Jesus tells the people they will "perish" if they do not repent. What can he mean by this? That God will strike them dead if they don't repent? I don't think so. That if we do repent we will escape physical death? I don't think so.

I think by "perishing" Jesus means not that we will be punished with physical death, but that we will never become the free and whole human beings we are meant to be. We will be like the fig tree that bears no fruit. We will not be fully alive. This is the sense in which we will perish. Think of it: if we never repented anything we had done or failed to do, who would we be?

Let's do a thought experiment. Suppose we do succeed in denying to ourselves the significance of our own sins, our own failures to live out of the spirit of love and life that we call God. What will happen to us? I think the knowledge will fester within us, like pus. Somewhere deep within us we will know what we have done, or failed to do, and find it intolerable.

What then? We shall do what people generally do: we shall externalize our sense of wrong and sin by placing it on someone else. We shall dip the brush in our own hearts and paint others with the color we find there. In an extreme case, the effect will be to make us feel entitled to attack, to wound, to torture, to kill those whom we have vested with our own failings, our own guilt.

Is this too extreme? Let me ask you this: what do you think is the fuel that all these years and centuries has fed the flames of white racism in this country, leading in the past to slavery, Jim Crow, lynching, and in our own time to the racism with which we are so familiar, including such things as the abandonment of poor people of color as though they do not matter?

I am sure that a part of it is that at some level the slave owner knows that it is human beings he is claiming to own, human beings he is depriving of the fruits of their own labor, human beings he is starving and abusing and humiliating and torturing. He knows that this is a monstrous sin. But he denies it all; he finds a way to cover it with another ideology, including a religious ideology, which justifies it. He believes his own propaganda. He lies to himself, and he pays the price. He is spiritually and psychologically deformed. He falls into a kind of fundamental incoherence.

In the language used by Jesus in the gospel today he perishes. For this is what Jesus means by perishing: not physical death but the death of the soul.

If he could admit this crime, confess it, repent it, and ask forgiveness for it, real good might come to him. In my time I have known white people in my generation from the South who did not deny, but admitted, who did not sweep away, but faced, what all this means and where it comes from, and their own implication in it. As a result they were in a completely different psychological and spiritual state from those who inherited denial as the curse of the slave owner. You could see it instantly in their faces, in the way they stood and moved; you could hear it in their voices, in their laughter. They will not perish. Not ever. I admire them beyond words.

Now the white slave owners were not born bad people. They were born, like all of us, into a particular culture and society, which, together with their own human selfishness, did much to form them. What they became first as slave owners, and in subsequent generations simply as racists, was the predictable result of being born as human beings into that corrupt world. What they became is their punishment.

I think Jesus is telling us that we are all like white southerners, even if we are not white, even if we are not southerners, for we are all born into a corrupt world that has to some degree shaped us. And we are all selfish. None of us loves God with our whole hearts or loves our neighbors as ourselves, as we confessed this morning. We all need to be freed from the sense of fault and wrong we know in our hearts, but deny in our minds and voices.

I think this freedom can be ours not by a blanket absolution, or by the simple assurance that God loves us all, but only by the process that

Jesus invokes: the recognition of evil within us, the confident asking of forgiveness, and the acceptance of that forgiveness when it is given. This is what he is telling the people to do.

Of course our repentance can never be perfect. It is not like baptism, to be done once and for all. It is a practice that needs to be a part of life, like the other practices of our worship together, such as the Penitential Order with which our service today began.

You will have noticed that I have been talking about white southerners almost as if they were alien creatures, far worse than we are—as if they were the Galileans in our story who supposedly deserve whatever they get. I have been drawing a line between us and other human beings.

When I do that I am doing exactly what Jesus rebukes the people for doing, which is to deny my connection with another by thinking that I am morally superior, hence morally safe. Which I am not. I have been talking about white racism in a self-righteous way, but the truth is that whatever I do to rid myself of it, to my horror I still discover, from time to time, shreds and pieces of it within me. This may true of all white people raised in this country. None of us can escape our implication in a system of racial oppression. And those of us who do not have this particular problem have other respects in which we fail as loving people. All of us.

So what are we to do? How are we to live on these conditions?

Jesus does have an answer—incomplete, but an answer. What he is telling people like me, and you, and all of us, is something like this.

"Stop your worrying about how bad *they* are, those slave owners and racists and other people who live in denial of their own wrong. Worry about yourself. You sin too. Worry about your own betrayals of the Spirit of Love, about your own denials of those betrayals, about your own heart and soul. Have the strength to ask for forgiveness, and the strength to accept it when it is granted.

"Do not say No to the great and gracious gift you are offered, the gift of repentance and forgiveness, the gift of reconciliation. Accept this gift and you will not perish. You will flourish and bear fruit in who you are and what you do."

Jesus is showing us the way in which we can be brought to share the life that is eternal, the life of health and love and truth. It is a sacrament. In fact he is trying to bring us to that life: to feed and nourish us, like the fig tree, for another year, in the hopes that we can bear the fruits of repentance, forgiveness, and growth into union with the God of Life.

AMEN

Questions

1. Have you ever repented of wrongdoing or sinfulness? What was that like? What did the experience lead to?

2. Think of the general confession, in which we do formally repent and ask forgiveness of God. What is it like for you to say those things? What has it led to in your life?

3. Can you imagine repentance as a source of deep joy? I was once walking down the nave of a church in Italy, away from the altar, when I saw a woman enter the church with an eager stride, looking roughly in my direction. Her face was immediately illuminated by a wonderful smile, confident and joyful. I turned to see what or who she was smiling it, and behind me I saw her confessor, walking towards the confessional booth she was approaching, and smiling at her. She was coming to her confession with confidence and joy. Can you imagine doing that?

4. Have you ever experienced the festering power of unrecognized sins, in yourself or others?

5. As you think about the gospel passage we have read, what prayer do you find yourself wishing to make?

29

The Resurrection of Jesus

This sermon was given at the Easter Vigil, the service that takes place on the Saturday night before Easter Day. This is the moment when the Resurrection of Jesus is celebrated. We begin in the dark, and when the Resurrection is proclaimed we go in a moment from the darkness of Lent to the light of Easter. The altar, which had been stripped, is now made an altar again, with fresh cloths and flowers. We sing one of the favorite hymns of Easter, "Jesus Christ Is Risen Today," and shout out "Hallelujah," a word that is by tradition never uttered during Lent. This is a great moment.

The questions it presents are hard, maybe the hardest and most important questions for any Christian. What is the Resurrection? Did it really happen? Does it matter if it did not? Perhaps you should take a little time to think about, even to write down, what you think about these things, before going further.

The Gospel of Matthew 28:1–10

After the Sabbath, as the first day of the week was dawning, Mary Magdalene and the other Mary went to see the tomb. And suddenly there was a great earthquake; for an angel of the Lord, descending from heaven, came and rolled back the stone and sat on it. His appearance was like lightning, and his clothing white as snow. For fear of him the guards shook and became like dead men. But the angel said to the women, "Do not be afraid; I know that you are looking for Jesus who was crucified. He is not here; for he has been raised, as he said. Come, see the place where he lay. Then go quickly and tell his disciples, 'He has been raised from the dead, and indeed he is going ahead of you to Galilee; there you will see him.' This is my message for you." So they left the tomb quickly with fear and great joy, and ran to tell his disciples. Suddenly Jesus met them and said, "Greetings!" And they came to him, took hold of his feet, and worshiped him. Then Jesus said to them, "Do not be afraid; go and tell my brothers to go to Galilee; there they will see me."

The Church of the Incarnation, March 30, 2013

May the words of my mouth and the meditations of my heart be always acceptable in thy sight, O Lord, my strength and my redeemer.

This is the day we celebrate the Resurrection of Jesus, the moment at which our Lord becomes our Risen Lord. It is the most joyful moment in the Christian year and profoundly sacred. I hope we all feel the joy deep in our hearts.

But some of us at least may feel a kind of anxiety or uncertainty behind the joy, a doubtfulness that impairs what we wish could be uncomplicated rejoicing. The question lurking there for you, as for me, may be this: is the story of the Resurrection true?

This is what I want to think about tonight.

One commonly proposed solution is to say that the story of the Resurrection is both totally true and totally unproblematic. The Scripture says it happened this way, and it did. Jesus was killed, his body was dead, and then he came to life again in that body, the way Lazarus did. He spent another forty days with his disciples, and in his body then went to heaven.

There are lots of people for whom this response works. For them this is the Word of God.

Another often proposed solution is to admit that the Resurrection is not true, but claim that this fact does not matter at all.

The argument goes like this. It is clear that some of the disciples had a strong internal sense that Jesus was with them on certain occasions after his death. But that they had this feeling does not mean that Jesus really did come back to them after his death. The kind of thing the disciples experienced can happen in natural ways, and does not require the miracle of a person dying and coming back to life. It was perhaps a kind of hallucination, driven by the disciples' need and love and misery.

There are lots of people for whom this response works. For them this is the Word of God.

I don't want to criticize people for whom one of these solutions works, but neither of them works for me, and perhaps that is true of you too.

The heart of the difficulty is that both seem to pretend that something that is in fact deeply problematic presents no problem at all. Once we accept either of them, we are likely to think that we need no longer engage with the gospel text and the serious problems it presents to our understanding and our lives. We will have disposed of the Resurrection of Christ by putting it up on a kind of shelf in a closet, where we need not think about it anymore.

In this way both approaches seem to me to trivialize the event and the mystery it presents. They sweep away the very problems that it is the point of the story to force upon us.

Take the first solution. Although it claims to rest on a literal reading of the Bible, in fact it does not pay enough attention to what the gospel actually tells us: Jesus twice entered a locked room to see his disciples, passing through a solid wall; Jesus met the disciples on the road to Emmaus, shared a meal, and then disappeared from their sight; and Jesus somehow showed up miles away in Galilee, where he greeted the fishermen coming in for breakfast. In these accounts Jesus has a body, but a body unlike anything anyone has ever seen before, capable of instantaneous movement through space, through solid walls. It is an immense mystery.

The first solution wants to reduce a story that is full of mystery and wonder to an outline that obscures those things. It wants to normalize the Resurrection.

The second solution also wants to deny the mystery and wonder of the story, this time by denying that anything really miraculous happened. The idea is that what appears to be a resurrection is really just a familiar psychological phenomenon brought on by acute need and desire.

Like the first, this solution wants to substitute for the story actually told in the gospels a story of its own, a story that will make the mystery and wonder disappear.

Are these two solutions the only possibilities: what might be called objective truth in the first and subjective truth in the second? Or is there a more satisfactory response to this amazing story, a story that is in one sense both utterly incredible and in another sense more true than any other story ever told?

Let us start by asking ourselves what we might hope for in our response. Both of the proposed solutions seem driven by a desire to render the story comfortable and nonproblematic. But I think this very effort is a mistake, for it misunderstands and frustrates the nature of Scripture, which constantly presents us with problems and difficulties we do not want to face. Scripture does not resolve them or sweep them away, but forces them on us. That is its very purpose.

Think of the psalms, which combine some of the most beautiful images and language and feelings with horrific desires for vengeance and destruction. Think of the whole history of the people of Israel, whose relation with Yahweh is not comfortable or understandable on either side, but reflects the deeply troubling realities of human nature and the world with which we have to deal. Or think of Jesus' commandments to us, to love our God with all our hearts and minds and souls and to love our neighbors as ourselves, commandments none of us can possibly obey but which are immense gifts to us.

In these instances, as always, the tensions, puzzles, and contradictions of Scripture are an essential part of its truth. It is important to recognize that in talking to us this way Scripture is treating us with immense respect, for it is trusting us to tolerate the emotional and intellectual stress it creates. It is trusting us to live with contradiction, paradox, and mystery; indeed it teaches how to do those things.

Its point is never to simplify or make easy, but always to complicate and make hard. The Resurrection story is no exception.

I think the gospels are telling us that the Resurrection is real, mysterious, and problematic. It cannot be disposed of by simple belief or simple disbelief. It is there, before us, as a reality in the text and in the world. But what it is we cannot know.

In reading the gospels that tell of the Resurrection we are called to come to terms with the wonderful stories they tell, stories that neither of the proposed solutions takes seriously. Think of the empty tomb in Mark, Matthew's women in the Garden, Luke's road to Emmaus, the appearance of Jesus to the disciples in Jerusalem, John's story about Doubting Thomas, and the breakfast of fish by the Sea of Galilee. These are stories to be lived with, brought into the heart and mind. In my view they are stories to be trusted as the foundation of our lives.

We are right to trust them. We do not know what the Resurrection looked like in detail—how could we? It happened only once in the history of the world!—but if we read the text with an openness to its difficult truth it is clear that something happened to these people, something they felt to be world historical.

The gospel is telling us that what they experienced was not an hallucination, but the actual presence of Jesus; not just as an idea, but as a fact; not just once, but many times; not in one place, but in several places; not in individual visions, but in shared experiences.

This is what they reported to their friends, speaking the truth as well as they could about something they could not understand, and this is what their friends report to us in the gospels. We are told these things by witnesses we are right to trust.

The two solutions I mentioned earlier both want, in different ways, to drain the Resurrection of its mystery and wonder. But the gospels call us again and again to live with mystery and wonder. They teach us that it is in facing uncertainty and tension and contradiction, in confronting the limits of mind and heart and language, in living openly with mystery, that human life can be lived with the deepest connection to our God.

We actually know this is true from our own experience of life, though we usually push the knowledge aside, finding it intolerable. Mystery is in fact at the heart of our lives. Take the mystery of our own existence. Where did we come from? Who are we really? What do we see when we look deeply within? This is all mystery. Take the mystery of the people we know and love. Who are they? Who are we to each other? What is a marriage or a friendship? This is all mystery. Or think of the mystery of children, as new souls born into the world with lives of unimaginable meaning ahead of them, or of the mystery of death, as we pass one by one from this existence into something else we cannot know. Or consider the mystery of the life of our bodies, as we breathe and see and hear, indeed the mystery of all life on the planet. Everything that ever happens to us, everything we ever do, is embedded in mystery, and it is from mystery that it gets it deepest meaning.

As the first solution pays not too much, but too little respect to the Scripture it rests on, so the second solution pays not too much, but too little respect to common sense and ordinary experience.

The Resurrection calls us to live in awareness of the mystery of Jesus, in his life and in his death and in his new life among us now. That the Resurrection was and is a mystery makes it not less real than other events but more real, more full of meaning and significance.

I was talking with a friend by e-mail about these matters, and he said, in language upon which I cannot improve, that religious faith is never a question of asserting mere objective truth, or mere subjective truth (the way our proposed solutions do): "It always involves just the opposite of these things: participation, ethical response, passionate embrace, and liturgical remembering."

This is the kind of life to which the Resurrection calls us.

Look at the disciples and the kind of lives they led after Jesus appeared to them. In what they were able to achieve we can see the effect of the immensely transforming power of Jesus' presence with them. These unlettered fishermen, ordinary country people, were transformed by the Resurrection into phenomenally competent and active agents of God. They established and built up the church, the church that is still with us— this church of the Incarnation—which is something they would earlier never have dreamed they could do. Think of Thomas, sailing off to India to establish the church that still exists there.

Something mysterious and wonderful happened to all of them. It was not just that they grieved brokenheartedly for Jesus and wished he had not died. He was actually with them after his death. We cannot understand how this happened, and they could not understand it, but it happened.

In his Resurrection appearances Jesus showed them that they need not ever fear death, or anything else. They were freed and transformed to go forth as the confident and trusting servants of the Good News.

It was not only Jesus who was resurrected from death. The disciples were resurrected too, from a different kind of death, from their desolation and despair. And we can be resurrected too, from the deaths we experience in our own lives, from the worst death of all: from death in life.

Alleluia! The Lord is Risen indeed. Alleluia!

AMEN

Questions

1. Think about the mysteries upon which your own life is founded. Your own conception, for example, as a sperm entered an ovum; your own growth into a baby waiting to be born; your finding yourself in a new world, full of bright lights, in which you suddenly had to breathe air. And breathing itself, the process by which without our noticing it oxygen enters the blood and carbon dioxide leaves it. One could go on and on and on. Our whole lives are founded upon mysteries we cannot grasp. It is all an immense gift. Science can explain some things, but surely not everything. What do you feel as you contemplate this fact? Does it affect the way you think about other people?

2. Have you ever experienced or witnessed an event that has some of the quality of a resurrection? Think of deep transformations in your own life or the life of a friend. Have you ever had the feeling that you, or a friend, had been lost but were now found, had been a slave but were now free?

3. As you think now about the story of Jesus' Resurrection, how would you compose a prayer in response to it?

30

Jesus in the Locked Room

The gospel passage given below tells the famous story of Doubting Thomas. As you read it, imagine yourself first as one of the other disciples, to whom Jesus came while Thomas was away, and ask what you think and feel at every stage of the story. Then imagine yourself as Thomas and ask what you think and feel at every stage of the story. Then think of yourself as a reader, as a person in the world today, and ask how this story speaks to you. What is it asking you to become, to say, to do?

The Gospel of John 20:19–29

When it was evening on that day, the first day of the week, and the doors of the house where the disciples had met were locked for fear of the Jews, Jesus came and stood among them and said, "Peace be with you." After he said this, he showed them his hands and his side. Then the disciples rejoiced when they saw the Lord.

Jesus said to them again, "Peace be with you. As the Father has sent me, so I send you." When he had said this, he breathed on them and said to them, "Receive the Holy Spirit. If you forgive the sins of any, they are forgiven them; if you retain the sins of any, they are retained."

But Thomas (who was called the Twin), one of the twelve, was not with them when Jesus came. So the other disciples told him,

"We have seen the Lord." But he said to them, "Unless I see the mark of the nails in his hands, and put my finger in the mark of the nails and my hand in his side, I will not believe."

A week later his disciples were again in the house, and Thomas was with them. Although the doors were shut, Jesus came and stood among them and said, "Peace be with you." Then he said to Thomas, "Put your finger here and see my hands. Reach out your hand and put it in my side. Do not doubt but believe."

Thomas answered him, "My Lord and my God!"

Jesus said to him, "Have you believed because you have seen me? Blessed are those who have not seen and yet have come to believe." Now Jesus did many other signs in the presence of his disciples, which are not written in this book. But these are written so that you may come to believe that Jesus is the Messiah, the Son of God, and that through believing you may have life in his name.

The Church of the Mediator, April 7, 2013

May the words of my mouth and the meditations of my heart be always acceptable in thy sight, O Lord, my strength and my redeemer.

The story we just heard is one of the most beautiful and affecting stories in the gospel. Who does not identify with Doubting Thomas, and rejoice when his doubts are removed and his faith restored? We are all Thomas, and we know it.

But the Thomas story is only one of two stories told in the gospel today. The first one has to do with the other disciples, whom Jesus visits in the locked room on the day of his Resurrection. It sets the stage for the Thomas story a week later, but it also has a shape and meaning of its own, which it is worth tracing out in some detail.

First some background. As John tells the story, Mary Magdalene went to the tomb and, when she saw that it was empty, ran to Peter and the unnamed disciple whom Jesus loved, to tell them about it. These two men ran to the tomb, saw it was empty, then returned home. Presumably they told the other disciples that the tomb was empty, but they had no idea of a resurrection.

Meanwhile Mary stays weeping at the tomb. She suddenly sees two angels, who ask her why she is weeping, and she says, "Because they have taken away my Lord and I don't know where they have taken him." What she thinks is that the body has been removed, and not by a friend.

Then she turns and sees the man she thinks is the gardener, and asks him where he has taken the body. Of course this man is Jesus himself, who says to her, in one of the most beautiful moments in Scripture, just one word, her name: "Mary."

When she is named, she instantly sees and understands. She goes and tells the others what she saw and experienced.

This means that at the time the disciples are collected in the locked room at the beginning of today's Gospel, two of them have seen the empty tomb and the others have heard from Mary what she saw and heard.

This does not necessarily amount to much. The tomb may be empty because the body was stolen, as Mary thought, and as for what Mary has said to them, do they believe it? Or did she experience a kind of hallucination or fantasy? They do not know. This is the first fact about them. They know something happened but not what. They have not seen.

The second fact is that they have locked the door because they are afraid of the Judean authorities. Of course they are afraid: their beloved leader has been killed by order of a Roman official, and they are known to be his followers.

It is this fear that Jesus addresses first. He stands among them and says, "*Peace be with you.*" Peace is just what they do not have and most need, and his presence must have felt wonderful beyond words. Jesus then shows them his wounds, to establish that it is really he who is with them. They rejoice at the return of their friend and teacher.

Jesus repeats the phrase, "*Peace be with you,*" and then engages in a rather elaborate ritual. First he says, "*As the Father has sent me, so I send you*"; then he breathes upon them and says, "*Receive the Holy Spirit*"; then he tells them that they have the power to forgive sins, or to leave them unforgiven—a mysterious, even dreadful, power. He has commissioned them as apostles.

Notice that this process comes in stages: first, the disciples' fear; then the grant of peace; then the evidence of the wounds; then the rejoicing; then the repeated grant of peace, the breathing of the Spirit, and the grant of power to forgive sins. By these stages Jesus has turned this group of frightened friends, hiding in an upper room, into joyful, confident messengers, full of the Holy Spirit, charged with spreading the Good News.

This is what Jesus came to do, and he did it. No small talk, no explanations, no theology, but a transformation of his grieving friends into the founders of his church.

What about Thomas? He was not there. When his friends tell him about these events, he refuses to believe them, refuses to take part in the life they share, unless he sees and touches the wounds in Jesus' hands and side.

This may seem petulant or excessive on the part of Thomas, but remember that the other disciples had seen the wounds. Seeing the wounds was in fact an essential stage of the ritual of healing and commissioning Jesus created for them. So Thomas is saying, I missed an essential stage in the process you went through, and I cannot go on without it.

When Jesus comes back, a week later, it is really for the sake of Thomas. He shows Thomas his wounds and invites him to touch them. "*Do not doubt*," he says, "*but believe.*" Thomas does believe in Jesus. He trusts him. We see this, because once he has seen Jesus he does not need to touch him after all.

Remember the stages of the ritual: fear, peace, seeing, rejoicing, and commissioning. Thomas has been afraid; he has received the peace; he has seen; and now he rejoices, saying, "My Lord and my God." He has been brought by Jesus fully into the community of the disciples, to be sent out by him as he was sent by the Father.

At the very end Jesus says something to Thomas that brings us directly into the story: "*Have you believed because you have seen me? Blessed are those who have not seen and yet have come to believe.*"

What Jesus says here is poignant. He has been assuming that no one could believe without seeing, and his experience has confirmed it—in Mary, in the other disciples, and in Thomas himself, all of whom had to see before they believed. In fact he came back to enable them to see.

But now he thinks of the future, of people who will not have seen. He thinks of us and wonders, "Will they be able to believe?" It will be very hard. Maybe not. Indeed, how is it that we can we believe in what happened on Easter in Jerusalem, two thousand years after the fact?

The short answer is that faith is a mystery, an immense gift of grace. We cannot explain it, but perhaps we can say something about how that grace has worked.

One way is this: as the last sentence of the reading suggests, we have the testimony of the gospels, which of course did not exist in Jesus' time. The disciples saw the risen Jesus and told their friends what had happened, and in the gospels their friends have told us. This is eyewitness evidence, even if at one or two removes. In reading the gospels we are thus carried back in time almost to the events themselves. It is like having a time machine, or a tape recording from 70 or 80 C.E. We are right to trust this testimony.

Of course reading the gospels does not enable us to see Jesus, but we do hear him. For the gospels are not simply third-person narratives describing a series of ancient events. They quote Jesus and carry his voice, his speaking voice, directly to us, two thousand years later. His voice is as fresh now as it was then—just as a violin playing a Mozart sonata written two hundred years ago sounds as fresh and new as the first violin to play that music.

So we know Jesus this way. We hear his violin's voice, as fresh as a newly minted coin. "*Peace be with you.*" "*Blessed are they who believe without seeing.*" "*Love your neighbor as yourself.*" "*Sell what you own, and give the money to the poor.*" "*If a man strikes you on one cheek . . .*" "*Blessed are the poor.*"

One might claim that the gospel accounts are not trustworthy because they do not perfectly agree about all the details, but this fact, odd as it may seem, is actually a reason to trust them. Each of the evangelists had his own perception of the Resurrection and what it means, which he expressed from his point of view. This very fact makes their stories more believable than if we had only one story, told exactly the same way every time, just as would be the case in a law court today. Perfect agreement between stories makes them all sound cooked up.

The differences among the gospels have another effect: they do much to shape the way they work and the kind of conversation they begin in us. The very gaps and inconsistencies open up for us a kind of space we can fill out of our own faith and experience. It is as though we have four somewhat inconsistent maps to the same terrain, all helpful, none perfect, which are in this way telling us that we have to make our own maps.

So, too, with the gospels. We have to put them together and make sense of them, out of our own experience, each in his or her own way. Our gospels impose this responsibility upon us; they grant us this freedom. In this way we ourselves are part of the process by which belief is kept alive.

Scripture is one of the things that enables us to believe though we have not seen.

But it is not the only thing. In addition to the gospels, we have a continuous memory in the church going back all those years to the Last Supper itself, when Jesus established the Eucharist that we still celebrate. This sacrament has been celebrated every single day since Jesus' death and resurrection; today it must be celebrated thousands of times every day, maybe every hour, around the world. It is what Christians do.

Each celebration is directly connected to all the others, to all the other remembrances of Jesus' life and death and resurrection, running right back to the Last Supper. We have been saying "Alleluia! The Lord is Risen!" for two thousand years.

These are all ways in which we can believe and trust, without having seen.

But is it really true that we have not seen the living Jesus?

Not, for most of us, in the way the disciples did, that is, with Jesus as a living, embodied presence before our eyes. We each have different experiences of Jesus today, and these differences need to be respected. But I think there is one place where we can see him: in the faces of other people, especially those who are suffering. Jesus suffered on the Cross so that we would know that he was with us in our suffering. We can see him both in the sufferings of one another and in our own responses to them. Jesus makes holy the moment of human suffering.

I also think Jesus is present in another, much more joyful way, in every face of hope and trust—especially in the faces of children, whom he loved and respected so much. When we look into the eyes of a baby or a child, full of trust and hope, we are seeing the face of our Lord.

We believe because we trust, because we remember, because we have heard, because we have seen.

Thanks be to God.

AMEN

Questions

1. As you think about the gospel story from the point of view of Thomas, what do you think it means that in the end he did not have to touch the wounds of Jesus? He has seen, but he does not need to touch. Does this suggest that something like this might be true of us: we have heard and we have read, and we do not need to see?

2. What would it mean to "see" today? What would satisfy the doubter's need? If Jesus himself appeared before you, you might easily dismiss it as an hallucination, or, like Scrooge in Dickens's *A Christmas Carol* when faced with the ghost of his long-dead partner Marley, by attributing it to indigestion. The thought would almost certainly haunt you: how can what cannot be true be true?

3. As you think of the process by which Jesus led the other disciples from fear to full discipleship, can you think of any analogous processes of transition in your own life, or the lives of your friends? What are or were the stages of that process?

4. A retrospective question. In reading this book you have spent a lot of time thinking about the gospels, asking what they mean, and trying to bring them into your own life. What can you now say about the process in which you have been engaged? Has it been useful for you? How much have you yourself given it shape? How does this experience prepare you for your next engagement with a gospel text?

5. Has your theology—your sense of who God the Father is, who Jesus is, who the Spirit is, and what they want and how they work—changed in the course of your reading and thinking? How?

6. If you were to compose a prayer in response to the gospel passage we have been discussing, what would it be?

www.ingramcontent.com/pod-product-compliance
Lightning Source LLC
Chambersburg PA
CBHW070250230426
43664CB00014B/2473